THE CENTERS OF CIVILIZATION SERIES

(Complete list on page 175)

Dijon and the
Valois Dukes of Burgundy

Dijon and the Valois Dukes of Burgundy

by William R. Tyler

UNIVERSITY OF OKLAHOMA PRESS
NORMAN

International Standard Book Number: 0–8061–0979–3

Library of Congress Catalog Card Number: 70–160507

Dijon and the Valois Dukes of Burgundy is Volume 29 in *The Centers of Civilization Series.*

To My Wife

INTRODUCTION

T HE aim of this book is to introduce the general reader
to certain aspects of life under the Valois dukes of Burgundy with which he may not already be familiar, and to
give him some idea of the character of their fifteenth-century
world and of the men who lived in it. We are fortunate in
possessing many accounts of men and events by contemporaries, and enough works of art from this period have
survived in all media to give us an idea of its aesthetic tastes
and achievements.

Whether in Dijon, capital of the duchy of Burgundy ("the
cradle and the springboard" of their dynasty, as a French
historian calls it), or in their northern possessions which
comprised substantially present-day Belgium and the Netherlands (which Shakespeare called "waterish Burgundy"), the
dukes lived in an atmosphere of wealth and ostentation. They
were generous patrons of the arts and insatiably acquisitive.
They liked to collect all that was most rare, rich, and precious
in jewelry, plate, tapestries, textiles, and sumptuously illuminated manuscripts. They loved to hold banquets, tournaments, and ceremonies of incomparable lavishness and of
often disconcerting—to some later critics objectionable—
fantasy.

Court entertainment on such a scale reflected more than
mere indulgence in a taste for luxury and display. It served
psychological and political aims, for it was intended to impress public opinion, to generate domestically and in other

countries a sense of the ducal wealth and power and thus to increase the prestige of Burgundy. It was an effective way of serving notice on the other courts of Europe that the dukes had the means as well as the intention of asserting themselves on the international scene and that there was no material reason why they should set a limit to their ambitions. The ducal treasure, moreover, had a more immediately practical *raison d'être* than merely to dazzle foreign envoys. It also constituted a form of savings account to be drawn upon as security for loans to meet special needs. In an age when the mechanism of credit was rudimentary, the dukes often had to turn to money lenders to finance military expeditions or costly ceremonies, at exorbitant interest rates. These bankers came principally from northern Italy, and the risks they took were frequently immensely profitable, as the famous painting of one of them, Giovanni Arnolfini, by Jan van Eyck suggests. By the middle of the fifteenth century, ducal revenues were probably running close to one million ducats annually. This was nearly equal to the revenues of Venice, four times those of Florence, and twice those of the Vatican. However, even this was not always sufficient to meet the mounting ducal expenditures, and the treasure stood ready to be drawn on as needs arose.

The dukes' highly developed instinct for public relations also prompted them to encourage and support writers to record their achievements and to describe the splendor of their court. The third duke, Philip the Good, created the position of *indiciaire* ("historiographer") for this purpose. To this happy inspiration we owe most of the minutely detailed accounts of the pastimes and pageantry of the Burgundian court. It is not surprising that chroniclers, whether official or not, but mindful of their own interests, should have emphasized those events which redounded to the duke's prestige or credit, while glossing over or sometimes omitting altogether those aspects which it would have been impolitic to record. An example of such discretion which is greatly to history's loss is one chronicler's alleged inability to remember what was said at the interview between Philip the Good and Joan of Arc after her capture, at which he also was present. Nevertheless, however inadequate the writings of the chroniclers may be as history by modern standards, they are a precious and abundant source of information on the customs, manners, and tastes of the times and on the personalities of the leading figures.

In addition to literary sources there has fortunately survived a vast quantity of documentary material having to do with the administration of fifteenth-century Burgundy, which has still been only partially tapped. The records of government of the four dukes, and in particular the series of accounts and receipts—central, regional, and local—testify to the efficiency of the ducal administration and constitute an almost inexhaustible store of factual information. The English historian Richard Vaughan estimates that a collected edition in print of all known fifteenth-century European chronicles would fit easily on the shelves of a medium-sized bookcase, whereas a printed corpus of documents of the period from Burgundy alone would fill an entire room.

Three *a*'s come to mind when we think of the four members of the younger branch of the French royal family who were the dukes of Burgundy: ambition, action, and acquisition. By successfully pursuing a policy of judiciously planned marriages combined with intrigue and diplomacy (backed, when necessary, by force), they expanded their possessions and their influence to the point where they were given political consideration equal to that accorded to the kings of England and France and the Holy Roman Emperor. By the third quarter of the fifteenth century, the possibility was generally recognized that the Burgundian state might become an independent "median kingdom" between France and the Holy Roman Empire. Some historians maintain that the attempt to reach this goal was doomed to failure from the start. Others, less inclined to a deterministic approach to history, have argued that diversity of peoples, language, customs, and local institutions is not necessarily incompatible with the creation of a viable political entity, witness the Habsburg and Austro-Hungarian empires. Indeed, it is on this assumption that the hopes for an increasing unity of Europe are today based. The catastrophic failure of the attempt of the ducal policy to achieve its ends invests the epic of Burgundy both with a meteoric quality in its pace, brilliance, and sudden extinction, and with an element of classical tragedy in the punishment of *hubris* by the gods.

In keeping with the general purpose of The Centers of Civilization Series, this book addresses itself less to the history than to the cultural and social aspects of the period. At the same time I have long been conscious of the fact that the historical role of Burgundy is relatively little known, even to people with a general interest in history, and that a somewhat greater degree of knowledge about its place in European history than commonly exists is required if the age of the Valois dukes is to be seen in perspective. "Many things familiar to you," once wrote Samuel Johnson to a friend, "are unknown to me, and to most others; and you must not think too favorably of your readers; by supposing them knowing, you will leave them ignorant." With this exhortation in mind, in the opening chapter I have attempted to provide the reader with a historical and geographical framework within which to place the various activities and expressions of life at the court of the dukes with which the subsequent chapters deal.

Life at the court of Burgundy was a particularly brilliant reflection of the contemporary civilization of northern Europe in a period combining extremes and opposites to a degree which it is difficult for our age to comprehend: it was both coarse and refined, both cruel and tender, both cynical and sentimental. Under the patronage of the House of Valois, both French and Burgundian, masterpieces of art were produced of exquisite simplicity, delicacy, and refinement.

The social values and outlook of later ages have led to censure of the dukes for their disproportionate wealth in comparison with the lot of the average man. This was also a characteristic of the age everywhere; but while the poor suffered then (as they do today, with infinitely less excuse for society), there is no evidence that they resented the splendor of the ducal establishment. On the contrary, people were flattered by the prestige such display brought to their rulers and to themselves as their subjects. Moreover, the economic level of the population of Burgundy, particularly in the great manufacturing and trading urban centers in the north, rose steadily in the course of the fifteenth century in spite of the hazards of war, famine, and pestilence. It should also be borne in mind that in those times man's cruelty and other vices were more obviously displayed and assumed a less hypocritical form than they do today. His pleasures too were those of a simpler, more primitive social structure in which life's contrasts were more brutal, less attenuated, less concealed. It is tempting but unprofitable to pass moral judgment on another age on the basis of the standards of value of our own, and to apply to it criteria which are irrelevant to the circumstances of its historical and social development.

This book has no pretension to scholarship and, apart from consultation of the chronicles, is not based on original research. That I should have written it at all is due in large measure to fortuitous circumstances, thanks to which I have since an early age had the opportunity of becoming familiar with the French province of Burgundy, its people, monuments, and history. It is over half a century ago that I first lived there, and I have clear memories of the first world war in the little village of Genay, near the lovely town of Semur-en-Auxois: the young men attending mass before going off to the front, and the grief of families when they learned that one of them would never come home again.

In the course of the years I have accumulated a number of books and some knowledge about Burgundy and have been especially drawn to the period of its flowering and expansion in the fifteenth century. However, I never seriously entertained the idea of writing on the subject, and was more or less pushed into doing so by my old friend, Walter Muir Whitehill, himself a contributor to this series.

I will be pleased if this little book occasionally serves to whet the appetite of the reader and to entice him into reading more deeply about the history of Burgundy. It is a rich and rewarding field, closely related to the spiritual, artistic, and political development of Western civilization in the Middle Ages; and it is relevant to the issues which preoccupy Europe today as she gropes her way toward unity. Cities such as Dijon, Beaune, Autun, Brussels, Bruges, Ghent, and The Hague all have a common link in their past: they share memories of the Burgundian rulers who, for a period of time, fashioned a common administrative framework within which populations with differing languages and economies moved forward together, and who laid the foundations of the modern states of Belgium and the Netherlands.

I am particularly grateful to Pierre Gras, director of the Municipal Library of Dijon, and to his assistant, Georges Garreta, for their generous help. I am also indebted to Pierre Quarré, director of the museums of Dijon, and to Jean Richard, of the University of Dijon, for the information they have so generously given me. I also wish to express my appreciation to Mademoiselle Marguerite Masson, former director of the Municipal Library of Beaune, for her assistance on many points. I owe a special debt of gratitude to George Wingfield Digby, Keeper of Textiles at the Victoria and Albert Museum, for the many helpful facts and suggestions he has brought to my attention. I also wish to thank Richard Vaughan, of the University of Hull, for his kindness in communicating to me certain ideas and references.

My thanks go to Merlin Packard, librarian of Dumbarton Oaks, and to his staff, for their help on bibliographical references. I am indebted to John Wilson, draftsman at Dumbarton Oaks, for his assistance in the preparation of the map. Last but not least, I wish to record the debt I owe to my secretary, Miss Marguerite Tise, who typed and retyped my manuscript with a skill matched only by her patience.

WILLIAM R. TYLER

Dumbarton Oaks
September 1, 1971

CONTENTS

SUMMARY GENEALOGY
(Burgundy and France)

Charles V
King of France (d. 1380)

Louis I
Duke of Anjou (d. 1384)

John
Duke of Berry (d. 1416)

Louis II
Duke of Anjou (d. 1417)

Charles VI
King of France (d. 1422)

Louis
Duke of Orléans (d. 1407)

Charles VII
King of France (d. 1461)

Charles
Duke of Orléans (d. 1465)

Louis XI
King of France (d. 1483)

Charles VIII
King of France (d. 1498)

Louis XII
King of France (d. 1515)

John II, the Good
King of France (d. 1364)

Philip the Bold (d. 1404)
  m. Margaret of Flanders (d. 1405)

John the Fearless (d. 1419)
  m. Margaret of Bavaria (d. 1423)

Philip the Good (d. 1467)
  m. Michèle of Valois (d. 1422)
  m. Bonne of Artois (d. 1425)
  m. Isabel of Portugal (d. 1471)

Charles the Bold (d. 1477)
  m. Catherine of Valois (d. 1446)
  m. Isabel of Bourbon (d. 1465)
  m. Margaret of York (d. 1503)

Mary of Burgundy (d. 1482)
  m. Maximilian of Habsburg (d. 1519)

Philip the Fair (d. 1506)
  m. Joan the Mad (d. 1553)

Charles the Fifth
  Emperor (d. 1558)

Margaret (d. 1441)
  m. William of Bavaria (d. 1417)

Jacqueline of Bavaria
Countess of Holland (d. 1436)
  m. John, Dauphin of
    France (d. 1417)
  m. John, Duke of
    Brabant (d. 1427)
  m. Humphrey, Duke of
    Gloucester (d. 1447)
  m. Franz van Borselen (d. 1472)

Dijon and the
Valois Dukes of Burgundy

CHAPTER I

Historical Antecedents

"Sum Burgundus ego, sed non me poenitet hujus
Nominis; quondam hoc Aquilas tremefecit et ipsos
Pendere Romanos insueta tributa coëgit."
("A Burgundian am I, but I am not ashamed of this
name; once it caused the Standards to tremble and
forced the Romans themselves to pay unwonted tribute.")

—Pierre de Saint Julien,
De l'Origine des Bourgongnons (Paris, 1581)

For some five hundred years before it acquired the name of Burgundy, that part of Gaul encompassing roughly the region of the headwaters of the rivers Seine, Saône, Loire, and Meuse had (thanks to the civilizing influence of Roman occupation) played an active and important military, political, and economic role.

Since earliest times trade had flowed, men had traveled, and cultural exchanges had spread along these natural arteries. This "world between the rivers, a little Mesopotamia," as a French historian calls it, consists of a complex of hills, plateaus, and valleys drained by waters flowing ultimately into the English Channel and North Sea, the Mediterranean Sea, and the Atlantic Ocean. It was thus predestined to be primarily a zone of transit, of communication between north and south and east and west. It is easier to describe its topographical features than to define its boundaries, for it has no natural geographical limits or defenses. On the contrary, it invites penetration from all sides. It can be compared with the hub of a wheel, whose spokes are roads and waterways. The tin route from the British Isles followed the valley of the Seine and pursued its way south by way of the Saône and Rhône valleys. This region, which was later to include the duchy of Burgundy, has also been likened to "a threshold which joins together rather than separates" the river basins between the English Channel and the Mediterranean Sea. Thanks to trade, the ideas and the art of the Mediterranean world early reached this heartland of Gaul. As recently as 1953, the necropolis of Vix, near the town of Châtillon-sur-Seine, yielded a magnificent Greek bronze vessel of the fifth century B.C., with rich decoration.

The historical entity known as Burgundy has varied in size and in geography. At certain periods before A.D. 1000, the name Burgundy was also applied to what are now parts of Germany and Switzerland. In the early part of the sixth century of our era, the king of Burgundy could travel uninterruptedly on his own land from a point some one hundred miles south of Paris to the shores of the Mediterranean and eastward to the Rhine.

The most advanced of the Celtic tribes which had peopled this part of Gaul since roughly the middle of the second millenium B.C. was that of the Aedui. Receptive to ideas from the south, to which they were naturally exposed geographically, the Aedui were among the first of the Gallic tribes to be influenced by Greek mythology. They achieved a leading position in the intellectual life of Gaul, and their Druidic schools were renowned. Their role of leadership was achieved more by political astuteness and opportunistic intuition than by military prowess. They have been described as "a curious people, ambitious, not very loyal, and close to the

Romans"—in other words, collaborators. Their capital was a fortress on the summit of Mont Beuvray, a tree-covered granitic mass nearly three thousand feet high in the region of the Morvan, not far from Autun. Excavations have revealed the high degree of artistic and technical skill achieved by the Aedui. Their jewelry was distinguished by the use of enamel as well as by the variety and beauty of its design.

Of the three other major Celtic tribes in this general area, that of the Mandubii has a particular claim to be mentioned because of the importance of its political and strategic capital, the *oppidum* of Alésia, on Mont Auxois. It had been a holy shrine from earliest antiquity and was a sanctuary of the Celtic people. In the first century B.C., its pilgrimage was already reported to be centuries old. By attributing the foundation of Alésia to Hercules, the Greek historian Diodorus Siculus implicitly recognized the venerability of its history. The population of these four main Celtic tribes has been estimated at something less than one and one-half million.

Threatened in the first century B.C. by the irruption of the Suevi, a tribe which had crossed the Rhine in force, the Aedui withdrew to their fortress, threw themselves on the mercy of Rome, and called upon the senate for protection. From it they sought and obtained the title of allies of the Roman people. Thus it came about that the Romans established themselves in Celtic Gaul, and that Julius Caesar crushed the resistance of the Gauls under their leader Vercingetorix at the siege and capture of Alésia, in 52 B.C. Caesar then spent the following winter at the Aeduan fortress.

The history of "pre-Burgundian" Burgundy was to be marked during the next five hundred years by its rapid incorporation into the Roman Empire, with all that this implied for its economic and industrial development, as well as for education and the arts. However, from the middle of the second century A.D. onward, the power and hence the authority of Rome were steadily ebbing following the incursions of the barbarians across the imperial frontiers, which reflected her increasing inability to assure the security of her outlying territories.

In the early part of the Roman occupation, the growth of trade required an expansion of the road system as well as the increased use of natural waterways. The geographic characteristics already mentioned of the region that was to become Burgundy had from early times favored the construction of a network of roads, to which the Romans now added their great strategic highways. These were not only responsive to the needs of trade but also facilitated the movement of troops, in case of need, for the repression of local uprisings or for defense against invasions from the East.

In 43 B.C., Lugdunum (Lyon) was founded at the junction of the Saône and Rhône rivers. It was destined to play a major role, both in the Romanization and in the Christianization of Gaul. In spite of occasional revolts in the first century A.D., whether due to resistance to the centralizing policies of the emperor or in protest against the imposition of taxes, steady progress was made in the integration of Gaul within a single Roman administrative framework. By the end of the century, the organization of the area in accordance with Roman law, custom, and authority had been completed.

Under the emperor Claudius (A.D. 41–54), the Aedui were admitted to the Roman senate. The leading Celtic families and public figures easily adapted themselves to the way of life and the customs of Rome. Under Augustus, the process of Romanization had been furthered by the construction of a new capital, Augustodunum (modern Autun) a few miles to the east of Mont Beuvray. Within a walled enclosure of over three hundred acres, which made it the third largest city in

Gaul after Trier and Nîmes, Augustodunum boasted the largest theater and amphitheater. It had temples dedicated to Minerva and to Apollo and became famous for its school of rhetoric and as a center of Roman education. However, it was at a geographical disadvantage, being neither close to any major commercial artery nor strategically located. In the second half of the third century it was sacked by the barbarians; and only a few years later the poet Ausonius, though of Aeduan origin through his mother, did not even list it among the leading cities of Gaul.

The decline of the power of Rome was accompanied by the creation of new territorial divisions. As in the case of Augustodunum, the large towns shrank and withdrew into themselves before the barbarians' onslaught. Concurrently with the undermining of the authority of the Roman establishment, a new institution was gradually making itself felt, slowly in its initial stages but by degrees creating the conditions under which the transition from the classical to the medieval world was to be achieved. From Lugdunum, where the first church was built in the second third of the second century, Christianity spread northward following the waterways and other channels of trade, withstanding persecution and penetrating the most remote areas. By the middle of the third century, Christian missionaries were swarming over the whole of Gaul. The first bishoprics were established in the beginning of the fourth century. The boundaries of the Christian administration became roughly coterminous with the territorial divisions of the empire—the limits of the dioceses conforming by and large to those of the Roman cities or townships, which covered extensive areas of land. Among the most powerful and wealthy bishoprics were those of the two ancient Celtic capitals, Langres and Autun. When Constantine the Great, who had lived in Trier for several years and made it the most powerful city in Gaul, visited Autun in A.D. 311, he found the Christian Church coexisting with the pagan schools of rhetoric.

Many of the early martyrs and bishops of this region bore Greek names, from which one may assume close links with the Christian East, not only in theology but also in the arts. Doubtless the Syrian merchants who plied the trade routes of Roman Gaul brought with them merchandise which reflected the new styles of the imperial courts of Ravenna and Constantinople. Saint Germain, bishop of Auxerre, who had been a Roman officer, died at Ravenna in A.D. 448, and his body was brought back to Auxerre as its final resting place. However, while Christianity spread, paganism continued to flourish locally. As late as the eighth century, the cult of Epona, the mother goddess of Gaul, still had its devotees at Autun. Gradually, Christian images took the place of pagan symbols, and Christian places of worship ousted the pagan gods from their habitations. By the time the "Burgondiones" settled in the area to which they were to give their name, the Church of Rome had already created the organization and the religious framework within which the newcomers were to be peacefully absorbed.

Who were these Burgundians and where did they come from? It is at present generally accepted that they were originally a Scandinavian people inhabiting part of what is now southern Sweden, and that they started migrating southward at some time during the first millennium B.C. because of drastic changes in the climate, from generally dry and warm to wet and cold. Their pasture land gradually turned into swamps, their farm land into marshes. With no herds or crops, the population eked out a precarious livelihood by hunting and fishing, until finally it yielded to the urge to search elsewhere for a more favorable climate. Their name is associated with that of the island of Bornholm, in the Baltic Sea, some twenty-five miles south of the Swedish coast, whose name in the earliest records forms variations of "Burgundarholm," derived from *borg*, "high place" or "plateau" (justified by its rocky cliffs as seen from the mainland) and *holm*, "island." Archaeological evidence has been adduced to support the theory that the island gave its name to a tribe coming from the north about 200 B.C., of which a part continued its migration southward toward the end of the first century of our era, occupying the region between the Oder and Vistula rivers. The flow from Scandinavia to the Continent was not, however, restricted to those who passed through the staging area of Bornholm. Migration occurred also by the direct overseas route, so that the Burgundians were progressively reinforced as they pursued their turbulent course into the hinterland of the Continent, where they underwent varied and often catastrophic experiences. They are first mentioned by Pliny the Elder and Tacitus as members of the Vandal federation.

Their reputation in history is free from the connotations of brutality and destructiveness which are associated with the Vandals and other Germanic tribes. In the third century they pursued a southwesterly course and, after suffering severe military defeats, reached the Main River valley. In the year 406 the Vandals and some other tribes passed the Rhine, and in the following year the Burgundians followed in their wake, settling in the region of Worms. Having unwisely violated the Roman injunction not to expand further, many of them were massacred in 436 by the Huns, whom the Romans had launched against them. Their king, Gunther, was killed, this episode being commemorated in the *Song of the Nibelungs*, which is the name of the Burgundian clan to which the royal family belonged.

In 443 many of them were forcibly deported to the province of Sapaudia (Savoy), their capital being Geneva. In the years that followed they continued their peaceful infiltration westward and southward along the Rhône valley as well as northward up that of the Saône. As allies of the Romans, they represented to the local Gallo-Roman population a measure of security and protection against other more warlike barbarian tribes. Their settlement in the general area which came to be known as Burgundia was facilitated by grants of land and financial concessions by their hosts. By 470 they had occupied Lyon and were continuing to expand southward. To the north, they had taken over Dijon by 479, and by the end of the century the kingdom of Burgundy extended to the shores of the Mediterranean.

There are contemporary accounts of the difficulty with which the relatively refined Gallo-Romans adjusted to the presence among them of these amiable green-eyed giants with blond hair, which they washed with lime and rubbed with rancid butter. They were also prone to sing raucously under the influence of drink. Their number was probably small, having been estimated at a few tens of thousands or possibly even less. They were Christians, but their king, Gondebaud, had adopted the Arian heresy which the Goths had propagated widely. This as well as their territorial expansion led to conflict with the Franks to the north, whose king, Clovis, had been converted to orthodox Christianity. In the year 500 a major battle took place near Dijon, possibly near the present village of Fleurey-sur-Ouche, in which Gondebaud was defeated, though not decisively. In 506 he and Clovis signed a treaty of alliance which settled the political and territorial authority and scope of the kingdom of Burgundy. In 507 the name Burgundia appears for the first time in a letter of Theodoric the Ostrogoth.

In the history of the next five centuries the year 843 is particularly significant, for it was then that the Carolingian empire was divided up among the three grandsons of Charlemagne. Lothair, who assumed the imperial dignity, acquired a long and narrow central strip of territory running from Friesland to a point south of Rome. It included the capital, Aix-la-Chapelle, Lorraine (which derives its name from his), and a large portion of the old kingdom of Burgundy.

This was the genesis of the idea of a "median kingdom" which has managed to survive through the centuries and which seemed about to become a political reality under the Valois dukes. In a speech at Dijon to the Estates of the duchy in 1474, Charles the Bold alluded to "the ancient kingdom of Burgundy, which those of France have long usurped, and made into a duchy, which all subjects must deeply regret." The hint was clear that he had it in mind to remedy this state of affairs. Less than two years later he told the people of Nancy, the capital of Lorraine, that he envisaged that town as the capital of the independent state of Burgundy. Alsace and Lorraine formed geographic links between the northern and southern territories of the dukes. It was the attempt to control these areas which led Charles the Bold into disastrous involvement with the Swiss Confederation and ultimately to his defeat and death before Nancy in 1477. Even though an independent median state was never to come into being, the idea itself remained alive, and was even advocated by Himmler in 1943 as an element in the reorganization of Europe after the victory of the Third Reich.

In spite of the turmoil caused by the invasions of the Lombards, the Saracens, the Normans, and the Hungarians, and the absorption of "Burgundia" into the Frankish empire, a Burgundian identity survived and acquired increasing political recognition under the Capetian dukes of Burgundy (1032–

1361). Under these able and energetic princes, the territorial and political consolidation of the duchy was achieved and Burgundy played an incomparable role in medieval Christendom. It is tempting to see a connection between the concentration in our "little Mesopotamia" of monks fleeing in the ninth century before the Norman invaders who sailed up the rivers looting and burning towns and monasteries as they went, and the extraordinary vitality and expansiveness of religious life and art in Burgundy following the founding of the great monastery of Cluny in the first quarter of the tenth century. Within two centuries Europe, from the shores of the Atlantic to beyond the Danube and from the Baltic to the Mediterranean, was dotted with hundreds of Cluniac and Cistercian monasteries. Burgundy had become the fountainhead of the monastic communities of Europe and the chief uniting factor in the Christian world of the West.

Dijon only started to assume the role of the principal town and seat of the government of Burgundy in the tenth century, when the counties of the Carolingian administration were being consolidated into a duchy. Founded in Roman times as a fort and trading post, Castrum Divionense (Dijon) was first described by Gregory of Tours in the sixth century, in his *History of the Franks*, as having walls thirty feet high and fifteen feet thick, with thirty-three towers and four gates. He noted the fertility of the soil and the abundance of water which provided quantities of fish and turned the wheels of the mills. It was then not yet a city. It lay within the diocese of Langres, whose bishops had resided in Dijon since the previous century.

To the west of the fort was a cemetery containing the tomb of Saint Benignus, reputed to have brought Christianity to Dijon under Marcus Aurelius and to have suffered martyrdom, who was venerated by the local population. Over his tomb the bishops of Langres had built a basilica in the early fifth century, and a monastic community established itself next to it. The increasing political importance of Dijon was recognized by the abbot of Cluny, who, in the year 1002, sent a northern Italian monk, William of Volpiano, to build a new basilica there and to found an important monastery. In 1016, the year of the consecration of William's basilica, the bishop of Langres ceded Dijon to the king of France, Robert the Pious, but it remained within the diocese of Langres until 1731, when it became the seat of an independent bishopric. In 1032 the younger son of Robert the Pious became the first duke of the Capetian line. It grew in wealth and importance as the capital of the duchy and received a communal charter in the late twelfth century.

If the king of France, John the Good, had retained the duchy as part of his kingdom in 1361 when the Capetian line became extinct, his successors would have been saved much trouble and the history of Europe would have taken a different course. However, three hundred years of ducal rule had created a strong sense of political identity and local autonomy among the Burgundians. They immediately showed themselves to be extremely sensitive to the danger of the loss of their privileges and status through a takeover by the French crown. When John the Good named his youngest son, Philip, duke of Burgundy, he was responding to valid political exigencies; and he could not possibly have foreseen what was in store for his descendants, for the basis for the expansion of Burgundy to the north was laid by the marriage in 1369 of Philip the Bold to Margaret, daughter of the Count of Flanders. This proved to be the first installment in what a Dutch historian has called "a memorable story of fine diplomacy, high-handed enterprise, and good luck," which was to make the name of Burgundy loom large in the history of Europe for over a century.

CHAPTER II

Dijon Under the Dukes

W HEN Philip the Bold took up his residence in Dijon in 1364, the town contained within its walls two monasteries and seven parishes. The plans of the walls had been drawn up two hundred years earlier, but construction had lagged and they were not finally completed until the time of the first Valois duke. The area they enclosed was large enough to satisfy the housing needs of the growing population until the nineteenth century. They were strengthened by eighteen towers.

Although Dijon had many churches—which reportedly prompted King Henry IV to dub it "the city of the beautiful spires"—the number of its inhabitants was only about six thousand in 1436. By 1460, this figure had roughly doubled, thanks no doubt to improvement in security and general economic conditions following the end of the Hundred Years' War.

Of the many fine buildings which Dijon possessed in that period, three are worthy of special mention because they are closely associated with the Valois dukes: their palace, their chapel, and their final resting place. The town hall of Dijon now occupies their former residence, which was and still is the heart of the city. It is known that the dukes of the Capetian line lived on that spot as early as the twelfth century, and perhaps much earlier. It was built adjoining the old Roman *castrum* and within the northern defense wall, several towers of which were incorporated into its structure. Whereas

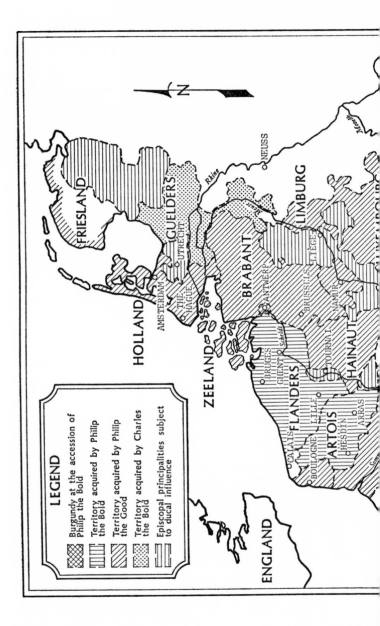

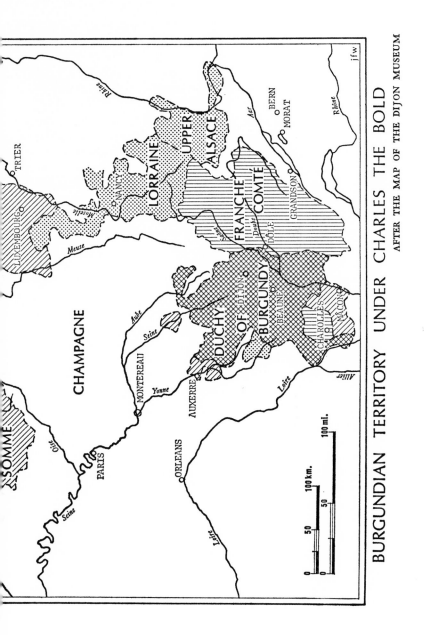

BURGUNDIAN TERRITORY UNDER CHARLES THE BOLD

AFTER THE MAP OF THE DIJON MUSEUM

the Capetian dukes had several residences, Philip the Bold was determined from the start that Dijon should be the capital of the new dynasty. He embarked on an extensive program of reconstruction and enlargement of the palace. He also founded a monastery outside the city walls to the west, to be a mausoleum for himself and his family. The oldest surviving portion of Philip the Bold's palace is a massive square tower known as early as the fifteenth century as the Tour de Bar, after René de Bar, subsequently duke of Anjou and king of Sicily. This gentle creature, a friend of the arts and later popularly known as *le bon roi René,* had the misfortune of being taken prisoner by Philip the Good and being incarcerated for a period of time in this gloomy tower.

Outside his palace, Philip the Bold also built a complex which included stables, baths, and housing for the ducal children. Direct communication with this group of buildings was assured by a bridge over a street. In the middle years of the fifteenth century, his grandson Philip the Good undertook an ambitious program of enlargement of his palace according to plans drawn by one Jean Poncelet who is also known to have worked on the tomb of Duke John the Fearless. Fortunately, in spite of additions dating from the seventeenth and eighteenth centuries and of vandalism under the Revolution, much from this period has survived. The ducal residence itself is still standing with its magnificent tower some 150 feet high. From it watch was kept over the surrounding countryside to warn of the approach of marauding bands which terrorized the region. The great hall of the palace, now known as the Salle des Gardes and part of the city museum, and the huge kitchens all bear witness to the scale on which the dukes lived and entertained. Philip the Good had plans, which he never carried out, to extend his palace eastward as far as the ducal chapel, already mentioned above. In 1460, he expressed the wish to be able to retire to his palace at Dijon, God willing, there to spend his declining years, but this wish was not granted to him. He died in 1467 in his northern possessions at Bruges.

The chapel of the dukes, later known as the Sainte-Chapelle, was founded in the twelfth century by Duke Hugh III in fulfillment of a vow taken while in danger of his life during a storm at sea on his way to the Holy Land. The charter, which has been preserved, dates from the year 1172. Dedicated to the Blessed Virgin Mary and to Saint John the Evangelist, the chapel (it is unfortunately necessary to write of it in the past tense) had the peculiarity of being "oriented" toward the north for reasons of convenience of construction in relation to the palace buildings. It was a long time under construction, not being finally completed until the end of the fifteenth century. Up to the time of the Revolution, it was intimately associated with the history of the duchy of Burgundy. In it were held the most solemn religious ceremonies and the funeral services of the dukes. When Philip the Good founded the Order of the Golden Fleece he issued letters patent establishing the permanent seat of the order in the Sainte-Chapelle. He also provided for a mass to be celebrated there daily, which continued to be the practice until the Revolution; and he increased the number of canons of the chapel to twenty-four to equal the number of knights originally admitted to the order. Each of the latter had his own seat in the choir of the chapel, and above it hung a painted panel bearing his coat of arms surrounded by the collar of the order.

In 1433, Pope Eugene IV, in gratitude for the support he had received from Philip at the Council of Basel, presented him with a miraculous relic from the treasure of the Vatican:

a consecrated Host on which was depicted our Lord seated on a throne. It had been punctured in several places by some impious hand, and from each hole blood had flowed. Isabel of Portugal, third wife of Philip, had a silver-gilt monstrance, with the arms of Burgundy and of Portugal, made for it. This Sainte-Hostie was venerated by the people of Dijon, together with the Romanesque seated statue of the Virgin which has survived in the church of Notre-Dame, and the relics of Saint Benignus. It was kept in a chapel of the Sainte-Chapelle named after it.

Curiously enough, the distinguished prisoner to whom we have already referred, René de Bar, while still incarcerated donated a stained glass window to the Sainte-Chapelle representing himself kneeling in prayer before the Virgin and accompanied by his protecting saints. According to tradition, René was not only a man of great artistic taste but also a painter, and it is considered plausible that he should have himself designed the composition of this window. The daily mass he founded for the Sainte-Hostie is represented on his own Book of Hours, which he possibly illuminated himself. In 1531 the emperor Charles V, who was likewise the duke of Burgundy, presented to the Sainte-Chapelle liturgical vestments which the king of Portugal had offered to the Order of the Golden Fleece. Additions and alterations were made in the interior decoration of the Sainte-Chapelle in the succeeding centuries, but when the Revolution came, this noble building was intact with all its contents, including the original heraldic panels of the knights of the Golden Fleece.

What happened then is described with painful precision by Pierre Quarré, director of the museums of Dijon, in the catalog of an exhibition held in 1962 of documents, drawings, and surviving objects relating to the Sainte-Chapelle: "After the confiscations of the Revolution, the statues were removed

to other churches, mutilated, or destroyed; the liturgical ornaments in cloth of gold, red damask, velvet, silk, satin of
Bruges, were thrown to the flames; the reliquaries, the goldsmiths' work, the liturgical objects of precious metal were
melted down and the relics cast to the winds. The 'Sainte-
Hostie,' which had been removed to the church of Saint-
Michel, was burned in public . . . and Isabel of Portugal's
monstrance was dispatched to the Paris mint. But the building itself had been spared. While most of the churches in
Dijon were restored to divine service after the Revolution,
the Sainte-Chapelle, the chapter of which had been dissolved,
was doomed to be demolished. The decision was taken in
1802 and immediately carried out by means of explosives: the
space was needed for the construction of a theater. By the
next year there remained only a pile of rubble of what had
been the finest Gothic building in Dijon, bearing witness to
the splendor of the achievements of the dukes of Burgundy
and of the monarchy, the seat of one of the most famous
orders of knighthood."

The forerunners of the Valois dukes were buried at the
monastery of Cîteaux, but in 1377 Philip the Bold decided to
found a monastery outside the gates of the town which would
play for him and his descendants a role comparable to that
of the monastery of Saint Denis for the kings of France. The
land was purchased in 1379; and in 1383, in the duke's absence, the first stone of the Carthusian monastery of Champmol was laid by the duchess Margaret, the second by their
son John, count of Nevers. The charter of 1385 provided for
a prior and twenty-four monks and stipulated that the monastery should be named after the Trinity. The duke had
chosen an order of monks "who night and day do not cease
praying to God for the salvation of souls, for the prosperity
and the welfare of the public weal and of the princes charged

with governing it." In his testament of 1386, Philip the Bold asked to be buried in the Carthusian habit and that wherever he might die, his body should be laid to rest at Champmol. His son and his grandson were also buried there; but the remains of the last of the four dukes were taken to Bruges. In his will of 1522, the emperor Charles V expressed the wish to be buried at Champmol, if the duchy had reverted to the House of Burgundy by the time of his death. Anne of Austria, great-granddaughter of the emperor, and queen of France, expressed the same desire.

For the plans of the new construction Philip called upon the architect Drouet de Dammartin, who had worked on the Louvre, and appointed him architect-in-chief. The church was to have a single aisle. To the west of the altar on the north side a two-story chapel was built as a private oratory for the duke and duchess, while on the south side a corresponding structure housed the sacristy on the ground level and above it the treasure room. Seen from the outside these architectural elements gave the church the appearance of having a transept. To the south stood the chapter house and the refectory of the small cloister. The large cloister lay to the southwest, and its galleries gave onto twenty-four little individual habitations for the monks, each standing within an enclosed garden.

By the time the church was consecrated in 1388, its decoration had only just begun. Claus Sluter, a native of Haarlem who had been working in Brussels, had been called to Dijon by the duke in 1385. In 1389 he was appointed to the position of official sculptor to the duke as successor to Jean de Marville. He transformed the design which the latter had planned for the west portal into a personal and original composition; in place of the traditional, static concept of standing figures of the duke and duchess on either side of the double doorway, with the figure of the Virgin and Child on the central door jamb, he created a larger, unified composition by representing the ducal couple on their knees, a guardian saint standing behind each one, and facing inward toward the statue of the Virgin and Child, in prayer. In addition to the decoration of this portal and the ducal oratory, Sluter composed and carried out a monumental Calvary which stood in the large cloister, its base rising from the waters of a spring—the symbol of regeneration. The Crucifixion with the figures of the Virgin, Saint John, and Mary Magdalen was destroyed at the time of the Revolution, but the base has survived and is one of the masterpieces of late medieval sculpture. On each of the faces of a hexagon, under enchanting figures of mourning angels with outspread wings, stands the powerful figure of an Old Testament prophet. Having foretold the New Testament, they stand there in witness of the supreme sacrifice of the Son of man. Fortunately, the head and torso from the figure of Christ on the Cross have also been preserved.

In the museum of the palace of the dukes at Dijon are preserved two monumental tombs, one of Philip the Bold, the other of his son John the Fearless and his wife Margaret of Bavaria. The base of each depicts the funeral cortege, in which mourners, robed in vestments with flowing folds and displaying demonstrative attitudes of grief, stand under arcades. Sluter and his nephew Claus de Werwe, who succeeded him after his death in 1406, were assisted by a number of sculptors from the Low Countries. By 1410, Claus de Werwe had completed the tomb of Philip the Bold. That of John the Fearless by the Aragonese Juan de la Huerta was not finished until much later, when Charles the Bold was already duke. He does not seem to have concerned himself with the idea of a funeral monument for his father, although the latter had arranged for the necessary materials to be brought to Dijon from Flanders.

A number of artists were also brought together for the pictorial decoration of the charterhouse. Like the sculptors, most of them came from the north. Philip the Bold ordered two large carved and painted wooden retables which were then brought down to Dijon from Flanders and installed in the church of Champmol. They are now in the ducal museum. They reveal the influence of Sienese painting, and it is probable that a polyptych by Simone Martini now divided up among various museums was already at Dijon by the end of the fourteenth century. Later, under Philip the Good, works by the van Eycks, Rogier van der Weyden, and other Flemish masters were added to those of the previous generation. Craftsmen in stained glass, metalwork, and in all other media were called to Dijon to carry out the sumptuous program of decoration. A *scriptorium* was established, in which the liturgical manuscripts required by the monastery were produced. This concentration of artistic activity made of Dijon at this time one of the major art centers of Christendom.

In the year 1390, when the program of decoration of Champmol was still in its earlier stages, Philip the Bold learned while in Flanders that King Charles VI was going to Avignon to pay a visit to the pope and would be passing through Burgundy. He hastened back to Dijon to supervise the preparations for the king's reception. First, he summoned the nobility of both sexes from the duchy and the county of Burgundy to Dijon. He had lists built for tourneys and jousts. These, together with the attendant facilities, such as tents, workshops, and stands, required much space. Given the church's disapproving attitude toward these knightly exercises, it must have been a particularly painful blow to the monks of the monastery of Saint Étienne to learn that the duke had decided that their *grand jardin* should be sacrificed for this occasion. The monks, however, were powerless in the face of the most formidable combination this side of heaven: the duke's will and the king's pleasure. All the trees were cut down, and the walls of the garden demolished—all for a visit of less than six days—for which loss the monks received five hundred *livres*.

While the construction of the lists was going on, the duke and duchess were hastily accumulating quantities of fine cloth: red and white velvet and satin for the knights, squires, and other officers whom the duke had called upon to be present, and cloth of gold for the ladies. All the men were to be dressed alike, as were the ladies. The duke, the other princes, and the knights were also to be dressed uniformly, half of them in red velvet and half in white; but the velvet for the princes was of finer quality and more beautiful than that destined for the knights. For the clothes of the duke and the princes, six measures were required, and thirty-six for those of the fifty-five knights. The squires and other officers were dressed like the duke himself in red and in white, but their clothes were "only of satin." The duke provided sixty-one measures with which to dress 122 squires. To each of the court ladies, the duchess gave a length of cloth of gold from which to have a dress made for the festivities.

Escorted by all the noblemen of the court, the duke and his heir, John, then almost nineteen, went to meet the king at Châtillon-sur-Seine and accompanied him back to Dijon, which they entered on February 7. The celebrations were endless: "Le duc y fit éclater sa magnificence (There the duke flaunted his splendor)," writes a historian. He presented the king and his brother with two fine horses each. To the duchess of Touraine, the king's sister-in-law, he gave a goblet and a water pitcher of gold. The base of the pitcher was studded with rubies, sapphires, and pearls, and on its lid were a large sapphire and six large pearls. He also gave her two rings, each with a big diamond. The duchess of Burgundy, too, had her presents ready: to the king a golden clasp set with three sapphires, two large rubies, and nine large pearls. She also gave him a large crystal drinking cup with a golden lid, set with diamonds, rubies, and pearls. To the king's brother she offered a ring with a large diamond. Five noblemen in the king's immediate entourage also received princely gifts from her. In addition, there was a general exchange of gifts. Members of the king's suite received presents of gold and silver plate. Before leaving Dijon on February 13, the king of France had the opportunity to admire the work that was going forward at Champmol. The duke accompanied him to Avignon where he stayed for a few days before returning to his capital.

Under the Revolution the charterhouse of Champmol was ransacked and almost entirely destroyed. Fortunately there have survived the west doorway of the church with Claus Sluter's statues; the base of the Calvary, popularly known as the Well of Moses with Sluter's statues of the Prophets, the fragment of the figure of Christ, and the tombs and retables already mentioned. A few other paintings and pieces of sculpture which have survived are scattered. Three statuettes of mourners from the tomb of Philip the Bold and one from the tomb of John the Fearless are in the Cleveland Museum of Art, and Jan van Eyck's *Annunciation* now belongs to the National Gallery of Art in Washington, D.C. "At the beginning of the nineteenth century," writes Pierre Quarré, "one could buy in Dijon paintings by Jan van Eyck, the Master of Flémalle, Rogier van der Weyden, or Simone Martini."

In contrast to the vision of beauty and splendor conjured up by accounts of courtly ceremonies and festivities, living conditions in Dijon in the Middle Ages were, as elsewhere, pestilential by modern-day standards. The two small streams which flowed through it, the Suzon and the Renne, fulfilled the role of sewers in spite of regulations and threatened penalties proclaimed by the municipal authorities. Within the town walls there was generally a shortage of water, so that what drains existed were flushed only when it rained hard enough. All garbage, except that thrown into the Suzon and the Renne, littered the streets. Manure heaps in the courtyards of houses and before their doors in the streets served as breeding grounds for flies and added their fragrance to the prevailing stench. The mind boggles at the thought of what life in Dijon must have been like in hot, dry weather, with the town shimmering in a cloud of iridescent and evil-smelling dust churned up by the inhabitants and thousands of dogs and farmyard animals. Philip the Bold tried to remedy this state of affairs. In 1390, he summoned his council, together with the mayor and aldermen of Dijon, representatives of the religious community, and the Chambre des Comptes to discuss a project for paving the streets. This was undertaken under the terms of a ducal decree. However, the financial support given by the religious community proved inadequate, and a more economical expedient was adopted: a deep trench was dug down the middle of each of the major arteries of the town, which was then filled with rocks and covered over with sand. This program dragged on for six years. By 1413 a start was made with a new program for paving the streets adequately. However, it also moved slowly, and it was not until the end of the seventeenth century that the streets of Dijon were properly paved.

The consequences of these unhygienic conditions for the

health of the population were severe: contagious diseases were endemic, including leprosy, said to have been introduced from the Near East at the time of the Crusades and which was to disappear only in the seventeenth century. In all this, Dijon was not unique. Paris itself existed in comparable conditions, scarcely imaginable to us today, and far removed from the idealized and romantic version of medieval life of a later age.

The houses which flanked the tortuous and narrow streets of Dijon were mostly wood; stone was not to come into general use until the end of the sixteenth century. The roofs of the more modest buildings were thatched with various grasses and reeds. Others were covered with thin slabs of stone (*laves*) still to be seen in Burgundian villages. This kind of roofing was extremely durable but so heavy as to require massive beams and walls for support. Finer houses had roofs of colored varnished tiles forming geometrical patterns, though this type of roofing was used mostly on churches, monasteries, and other religious buildings. One of the best examples of tiling to be seen today in Burgundy is the roof of the Hôtel-Dieu in Beaune, founded in 1443. Slate also was used, as on the roofs of the ducal palace. Some houses, as can be seen from a tapestry of the early sixteenth century in the Dijon museum, had stepped gables—an architectural element imported into the duchy from the Low Countries.

Every evening at sundown the bell of the church of Saint Jean tolled the curfew, and the sound of a horn warned the cutlers and armorers to stop their clanging and shut up shop. Lights gradually flickered out and shutters were closed. Save on special occasions, such as a fair or a ducal ceremony (when the inhabitants were encouraged to place lights in their windows), no lights were to be seen in the streets. Laborers in field or vineyard had to be back within the walls by nightfall or spend the night outside. One instance is recorded of a man who, finding the gates already locked, tried to crawl into the town along the malodorous bed of the stream Suzon and under the metal grill intended to keep out intruders. Unfortunately for him, the watch that evening was alert, and he was packed off to prison. Within the town, bakers, grocers, butchers, weavers, armorers, cobblers, locksmiths, leatherworkers, and all other tradesmen retired within doors, leaving the darkened streets to persons on special business, lawful or unlawful, or merely bent on the more or less dubious forms of entertainment provided by the various taverns of the town. Beggars and lepers found shelter in the two hospitals and in hostels for the sick. In spite of municipal regulations prohibiting any work between sundown and sunup, some inhabitants remained busy into the night, weaving, laundering, sewing, and generally catching up on their orders.

On certain feast days dancing in the streets in the evening was permitted. During Advent, the two town minstrels entertained the citizens at night with music and song as they marched through the streets. They were dressed in costumes chosen yearly by the town authorities (such as quartered green and red, as the records for 1458 tell us). Needless to say, the streets of Dijon were no safer at night than those of any other town of the period, and there were numerous disturbers of the peace. People who had to venture out of their houses usually carried arms as well as torches and, if possible, walked in company. It seems that Dijon, because of the fact that it lay on a major artery of trade, had a particularly large floating population of thieves, gamblers, adventurers, and scoundrels of all kinds, who hid out during the day and roamed the streets at night in search of an isolated victim, or of someone to fleece at the gaming table. Armed men in the service of some person of consequence would on occasion defy the night watchman trying to curb their rowdiness and put him to flight. In fact, the duty of night watchman, which each of the burghers of Dijon had to perform periodically, was no sinecure. Among the professional thieves and other criminals was a gang consisting, we are told, of "lazy vagabonds," who did nothing but eat, drink, and spend money freely and who, when they had no funds left, had recourse to various forms of mischief to recoup their fortunes. They were known as *les coquillards* ("companions of the shell") after the pilgrim's emblem of the scallop shell which they would sometimes wear in order to deceive their too trusting prey. It seems that François Villon may at one time in his life have been a member of this reprehensible gang.

Contemporary court records provide lively accounts of the goings on at night in Dijon. For example, on Thursday, June 22, 1464, "four or five companions with faces masked walked down the rue du Bourg . . . making loud mocking noises and committing several excesses and outrages, wandering through the streets of the town several times, and each time garbed differently—once in the guise of devils, shouting as horrifyingly as devils do in plays—from midnight until 2:00 A.M. They threw several rocks at shutters and windows, seized some wheels and some little barrels and piled them up on top of a well-head." They then tried to break into a house through the windows and scared the owner and his wife out of their wits by making fiendish noises and swearing in the name of the devil.

On August 15, 1473, the day of the feast of the Assumption, "the honorable man Jehan Aigneaul, burgher and municipal councilor of the town of Dijon that year, was carrying out the duties of night watchman . . . accompanied by his valets and some of his neighbors, in order to inquire and find out if there were any in the town making a nuisance of themselves or quarreling, or any foreigners, or others, for it is said that in this town there are often outrages, fights, and other acts of violence at night." About 11:30 P.M., as they were walking in the butchers' section of town (the rue du Bourg, always a center of lawlessness and disturbance), a butcher, Jehan Fèvre by name, snatched a torch and a stick from the hands of one of Aigneaul's young assistants, who had fallen behind the group. Aigneaul tried to get them back from the butcher while upbraiding him for being out in the streets at such an hour. The butcher, however, remained obdurate and refused to comply, whereupon Aigneaul seized him "in the name of the town." At this point, the commotion was increased by the screams of the butcher's wife and by the arrival on the scene of some of his neighbors, who, punning on the alder-man's name, shouted at him: "By the holy God, you shall not put him in jail, Jehan Aigneaul, Jehan Sheep, Jehan Ewe. Do we have to be governed by such a dyer?" (in the text *tainturier* or "dyer of cloth," presumably his profession). At this point Aigneaul thought it wise to release butcher Fèvre, who promptly went for him and seized him by the hair of the head, trying to throw him to the ground and to wrench his stick from him "in order to commit outrage on his person." The butcher and one of his friends were finally overpowered and thrown into prison. The next day, in contrite mood, they confessed their wrongs, the butcher explaining that it had been the feast day of his parish and that he had supervised a wedding in the course of which he had imbibed so much wine that he had been completely drunk. The town author-ities' hearts were not softened. Both men were heavily fined and made to kneel and pray and beg the mayor and the magistrates for mercy, heads bared, on the very spot where the outrage to the dignity of the town had been committed.

Bad boys would occasionally take advantage of the absence from town of a husband to try to force their way into his house, even having recourse to the subterfuge of pretending to be municipal officials in order to get someone to open the door. On August 30, 1447, a gang consisting of a notorious rowdy named Sancenot Bauchet, his brother, and two others, dressed in gray cloaks and dark hats, broke into the house of the carpenter Jehan Bougeot who was out of town. After beating up his wife Katherine, two of them raped her while the others stood watch and threw rocks in the street to try to drown her screams, making such a noise, noted a neighbor, that "it was as though all the devils of hell were present." Such was the terror inspired by this gang that none of the neighbors dared lift a finger even though they knew what was happening. Some women working at their spinning wheels nearby said afterwards that they had not dared stop spinning because of Bauchet's reputation, and it was to this that they attributed the fact that the gang had not stoned them as they left the scene of their crime even though they had been heard debating doing so. The gang was apprehended, nevertheless, and put on trial. One witness, who was a neighbor though evidently hardly a friend of the victim, while defending her conduct in general gave the following double-edged testimony. She made mention of certain factors which she seemed to feel might have been relevant to what had happened: "It is certainly true that since the said Katherine is given to laughing and is a gay wench, and has served as maid and nurse in various well-appointed houses in town, and knows a good many people with whom she frequently converses as they pass by in the street, calling them by their names—it could well be that certain evil people who like to speak ill rather than good, and who are delighted when scandals occur involving their neighbors, say that she is a woman of light virtue, and are suspicious of her." But, concluded this friendly witness, she "had never seen anyone entering the said Katherine's house other than her husband, who is a good man, and other people from among her household or her friends."

All through the fifteenth century efforts were made to improve the security of the Dijon streets at night. The rounds of the night watchman and the numbers of armed guards were increased, but in spite of these precautions, acts of violence continued to occur, so that in 1457 the night watchman was wearing "a steel bonnet" under his hat, to which he sometimes owed his life.

For the articles of luxury on which they spent huge sums, the dukes looked elsewhere than Dijon. For silks, cloth of gold, and fine fabrics they turned to Italy and Flanders, and to Paris and their northern possessions for jewelry, manuscripts, and works of art generally. Among the merchants listed as receiving large payments from the dukes we find some from Lucca, Milan, Germany, Ghent, Bruges, Malines, and Paris. Nevertheless, the presence of the ducal establishment with a large permanent staff and a continuing need for commodities of all kinds, whether the duke was in residence or not, constituted for the craftsmen and tradesmen of Dijon a steady source of revenue and an important market. Spices, cloth, wine, and a variety of agricultural and industrial products were furnished locally. As the names of the burghers in the contemporary local records are usually followed by that of their profession, the latter can readily be identified.

They fall, broadly speaking, into two major categories: lawyers and officials on the one hand, and tradesmen and merchants, who are more numerous, on the other—most of the inhabitants of Dijon in the fifteenth century were engaged in some kind of trading activity. In 1443, four thousand people were employed in the cloth business (about one-third of the entire population) as weavers, cutters, dyers, bleachers, bonnet-makers, and hosiers. Cloth manufacturing and marketing were strictly controlled by the town authorities, as were all other crafts and trades. They were grouped into *métiers* ("guilds") and subject to precise regulations and restrictions. Not only were technical processes of manufacture specified down to the last detail, including the grade and the quality of the raw material, but conditions of sale were closely supervised by officials under oath appointed by the mayor. In fact, our source for the number of people employed in cloth manufacturing and trade is a cloth merchant's appeal against a prison sentence he received for insulting a law enforcement official who was inspecting his business.

Thanks to the records and statutes of the guilds, we have a good idea of what the structure of the economy of Dijon was like in the fifteenth century. The more modest trades were those of the coopers, corkmakers, tanners, cutters, carpenters, cartwrights, ropemakers, and glassmakers. The élite consisted of first the weavers, then mercers, grocers, and goldsmiths and silversmiths. The butchers formed a particularly independent and powerful group which maintained its monopoly until the end of the century. Business was transacted in the many specialized markets of the town, to which thronged the farmers and peasants of the surrounding countryside to sell their produce and buy the manufactured articles they needed. There were separate markets for wine and for fish, while vegetables, eggs, and fruit were sold all together. We have already noted that the butchers had their stalls in their own part of town, the rue du Bourg, while at other markets wheat, cloth, and woven goods of all kinds were sold. These markets, however, catered only to local custom and did not attract individuals who were out to make a fortune.

Dijon also had two fairs a year, each lasting three days. They never achieved anything like the importance of the great fairs of Chalon-sur-Saône in the southern part of the duchy. The relative proximity of Dijon to the battlefields of the Hundred Years' War, and to areas where the dreaded *écorcheurs* ("flayers," murderous bands of discharged soldiers and thugs) roamed, discouraged foreign merchants from attending them. Later the provocative policies and bellicose activities of the last Valois duke also tended to keep tradesmen and customers away. One important source of revenue was the salt mines at Salins in the Franche-Comté. These proved extremely lucrative for able and enterprising officials and businessmen. The salt was sold to merchants who did not have the right to sell it retail, but had to deliver it to "salt warehouses," where ducal officials enjoyed the profitable privilege of selling it to the individual consumer.

All in all, Dijon was not an economically thriving town, especially when compared with the great cities of Flanders and northern Italy. Its principal asset was its role as the dynastic capital of the dukes and the seat of the monastery founded and embellished by them, rather than any noteworthy achievements by its population.

In Roman times Dijon had its *thermae* but it is not until the latter part of the fourteenth century that documents mention the existence of the ducal baths, the *étuves*. Rebuilt by Duchess Margaret of Flanders in 1384, they were housed in a square building surrounded by a gallery; the furnaces were in the basement and the baths themselves on the first floor. An external circular staircase led to an upper floor with several large rooms and an attic. There was a garden nearby with a well in it, which the duchess surrounded with trellis-work so that she could sit there protected from prying eyes. To make it possible for one to enter the baths privately and without having to cross the street, a gallery was later added to the second floor of the palace, which crossed the main courtyard and joined the bridge connecting the palace with the complex of service buildings. The gallery, roofed with the typical Burgundian varnished tiles, was of wood with stone columns. It was decorated with mural paintings and two windows provided light for it. A special niche hollowed out in the masonry of the steps leading down to the baths housed the duchess' pet hedgehog, which had managed to chew its way out of all wooden enclosures made for it. The rooms of the second floor of the bathhouse came to be used for guests of the ducal family, and when the future Charles the Bold, like his father and grandfather, was born in Dijon, these rooms were turned into a nursery for him for the first few months of his life. Philip the Good ordered a huge cauldron to be built for the baths, with a capacity of nearly 23,000 liters (about 6,000 gallons). By order of the duke it was filled and the water heated every month, a task requiring three days' work by six men and a tremendous consumption of wood, usually all for nothing since the duke spent less and less time at Dijon. While this wasteful practice was eventually abandoned, the bathhouse survived into the seventeenth century.

In the times which concern us there were also four public baths located in different parts of town, providing both hot-air and hot-water baths, the latter being more expensive. Both were totally devoid of any privacy, and this led to easily imaginable complications. In 1410, certain baths were assigned exclusively to men and others to women. Transgressors had to pay a fine—among these a monk of Saint Bénigne, discovered in the company of two married women. A couple of years later a new system was tried, certain days of the week being reserved for men and others for women. These measures served only to maintain the merest semblance of public order. The baths degenerated into centers of prostitution and noisy debauchery, with the customers drinking spiced wine on couches after their baths. A contemporary account notes that "there was such a noise of yelling, quarreling, [and] jumping up and down that it was amazing that the neighbors should be able to stand it, justice ignore it, and the earth tolerate it." However, attempts by the municipal authorities to correct these scandalous conditions were thwarted by certain influential persons. In spite of growing public reprobation and criticism, only superficial restrictions were imposed until the time when serious measures were at last taken to combat the indescribable conditions of filth already mentioned. It seems likely that the Italian wars of Charles VIII in the last decade of the fifteenth century opened the eyes of the French to the relatively far advanced urban and municipal programs of public hygiene in the towns of northern Italy. At any rate, it was in this period that the municipality of Dijon started issuing and enforcing strict regulations in protection of public health—among them a ban on public and private assembly and on heating the baths. The church also, sensitive to growing criticism of its role as the movement in favor of reform gained momentum, co-operated with the civil authorities in fighting crime and immorality. By the late fifteenth century, the public baths and at least the more notorious bordellos had been abolished.

As a center of travel, Dijon boasted a considerable number of inns, whose owners were not always above cheating the unwary traveler, as the municipal court records reveal. We read, for example, that on January 9, 1421, no fewer than six innkeepers, both male and female, were fined together on conviction of having given horses short measures of oats. They were also enjoined henceforth to utilize only official measures stamped with the arms of the town. One other case, brought up on the same day, involved a woman innkeeper accused not only of giving horses a short measure but of having added a double bottom to the measure she used. Her defense was that she gave them a heaping instead of a level cupful, but this was not found persuasive and she was also fined.

A more serious affair is recorded in the year 1455, involving an innkeeper, Étienne Penesset, landlord of "The Golden Eagle." One day in May of that year he had, while out of town, made the acquaintance of two Italian merchants, one, a goldsmith, from Genoa and the other from Lombardy. Having persuaded them to stay at his inn, he then introduced them to a certain friend of his in a nearby village, from whom they purchased a number of gold pieces. Penesset then ordered from the goldsmith a gilt metal chain, the price of which was to be ten gold crowns. Thereupon he denounced the two Italians to the ducal prosecutor, accusing them of being "con men, forgers and parers of gold coins, who had in their possession a great quantity of gold parings, and makers of false chains . . . of imitation gold," etc. A municipal official was dispatched by the prosecutor to place seals on the closet in the room of the two merchants and to seize their horses.

The innkeeper had in the meantime told the merchants that they had better escape, leave everything behind, and never come back, because if they were caught they would be thrown into prison, tortured, and "made to drink so much vinegar that they would take leave of their senses and finally be taken to the gallows and hanged there." Not unnaturally, the two Italians did not wait to hear more, but had the presence of mind to take sanctuary in the hospital of the Holy Ghost, outside the town walls. When he heard of this, the innkeeper was not at all pleased. He went to see them and tried to browbeat them into giving themselves up. Having failed, he got someone else to threaten them and try to scare them into leaving town altogether and for good, going so far as to offer to give their horses back to them, even though they had been impounded.

Being foreigners and knowing no one other than the innkeeper, of whom they were afraid, the two Italians were tempted to follow his advice. However, having clear consciences, they decided to fight it out and had the happy inspiration of appealing to a compatriot of theirs, a celebrated professor of law, whom Philip the Good had personally appointed to a chair in his recently created university in the relatively nearby town of Dole. From that moment on the tide of fortune flowed in favor of the innkeeper's victims. When the seals were officially lifted from the closet in the inn, it was discovered that part of the contents were missing. The innkeeper's defense was wholly unconvincing, but fortunately for him, his father managed to settle the matter out of court with the two Italians, and this, combined with a technicality enabling him to invoke the jurisdiction of another prosecutor than the one at Dijon, resulted in his getting off scot free.

In Burgundy as elsewhere in Europe, the origins of medieval education may be traced back to the monasteries, thanks to which the discipline of learning and our classical heritage were maintained and transmitted through the centuries. Schools were at first exclusively religious in character, their principal function being to turn out priests and clerical personnel generally. In the course of the Middle Ages scholarly institutions were increasingly secularized, the process being more or less completed by the end of the fifteenth century. In the early eleventh century the abbot of Saint Bénigne, William of Volpiano, founded a school and encouraged teachers, thus making Dijon a center of education and learning of the duchy, together with Châtillon and Cluny. The process of the secularization of schools, launched by the Lateran Council of 1179, was accelerated by the granting of an increasing number of communal charters and by the growing trend toward municipal autonomy. By the fourteenth century, not only the major urban centers but also a number of rural communes in Burgundy had lay schools. By the end of the same century, Dijon had a girls' school with a headmistress who was also authorized to teach boys. At the end of the thirteenth and the beginning of the fourteenth century Dijon had four different kinds of educational institutions. First, there was the school of the ducal chapel which provided both primary and secondary education. The existence of this establishment was an object of jealousy and resentment to the bishop of Langres, in whose diocese Dijon lay. He looked on it as a kind of unfair competition, even though the ducal chapel was not within his jurisdiction but was directly subordinate to the Holy See. Indeed the bishop went so far as to threaten with excommunication anyone attending schools other than those over which he had authority. The second type was the school of theology run by the Dominicans. Thirdly, there were two schools run by the bishop of Langres, which taught chiefly philosophy, mathematics, and grammar. Finally, there were some small private schools where the rudiments of law were taught by *legum professores*, who were not, however, members of a university faculty. Their teaching served largely to qualify students for posts in the ducal administration. Those who wished to pursue their legal studies went on to Paris or to Bologna, Italian universities being generally greatly in favor.

In 1332 the bishop of Langres succeeded in his efforts to establish his control over the ducal school, which was then brought under the same administration as the town schools.

Primary education in fifteenth-century Dijon consisted of reading, writing, and elementary mathematics, the study of the Psalms and, sometimes, of Latin grammar according to the treatise by Donatus. School children practiced reading with tablets on which were inscribed the various elements of grammar, prayers, and texts of Psalms. The classroom walls served as a blackboard; for writing materials the children used fine sand and fragments of slate, while calculation was taught with pebbles.

School teachers' pay was so modest that it had to be supplemented by other means, such as copying and illuminating manuscripts, for which, as we shall see in a later chapter, there was a constantly increasing demand from the duke and his court. In this way a *scriptorium* occasionally came into being in the vicinity of a school. As pupils advanced, the curriculum was broadened. Everything had to be memorized. After the age of twelve and in any case before the age of fifteen, the pupil also studied rhetoric, philosophy, and logic. The last, then considered the highest pinnacle of learning, was referred to as "the science of sciences" and "the art of the arts." Grammar was considered inferior to logic, as implied by the saying of the time, "Good grammarian, poor logician." Examinations took the form of discussions in which the student had to acquit himself honorably in order to obtain his baccalaureate.

In the early fifteenth century the schools of Dijon had achieved the status of a university, with a rector, six regents, and a faculty. The bachelor degrees it conferred were recognized by the Faculty of Arts of the University of Paris, though they were not considered equivalent to the degree of master of arts of Paris. It was to Paris that students went to acquire degrees of higher learning, but the possibility of fulfilling at Dijon the academic requirements of the University of Paris through the degree of bachelor of arts greatly contributed to the growth and the fame of the Dijon schools. Students flocked there, not only from within the duchy but from the Franche-Comté, Lorraine, Flanders, Switzerland, and Germany. Their number is estimated at one period to have reached two thousand. The schools also served as a source of teachers for schools in the surrounding countryside and in other provinces.

Another factor which may have favored Dijon as a center of education was the chaotic situation in Paris following the assassination in 1407 of the duke of Orléans by henchmen of John the Fearless and the resulting war between the followers of the former and the Burgundians. For the next dozen years, it was undoubtedly safer to study in Dijon than in Paris. Furthermore, the papal schism had split the faithful into two camps, France following the Avignon pope, and Germany the Roman one, with German students avoiding Paris as a result because of the number of Avignon clergy there. Instead they went to Dijon to learn French.

In 1424, Philip the Good founded the University of Dole in the Franche-Comté, which drew many foreign students, both because of its novelty and because it was farther removed than Dijon from the general area of military operations. Competition ensued between Dijon and Dole with mutual raiding of each other's students.

The highest official in the school system of Dijon was the choirmaster of Langres. All the schools' staffs owed him canonical obedience, and he alone was empowered to modify the statutes. Though not explicitly empowered to do so, the municipality of Dijon played a very active role in the administration and supervision of the schools through its control over the selection of the rector, or principal, and the code of behavior of the students. Since 1405 the municipal seal had to be affixed to all decrees issued by the rector and by other authorized school officials, thus in effect subordinating the rector to its control. Measures concerning the code of behavior and discipline of the students could be formulated and applied only with the mayor's approval. On taking office, the rector had to swear an oath to the mayor that he intended to discharge the responsibilities of his office loyally and to comport himself in conformity with the interests, the honor, and the benefit of the town of Dijon, as well as of the students. In fact, the imposition of the municipal seal turned the schools into an instrument of municipal privilege and power. For example, in 1449 the rector went in person, accompanied by clerks, to search the rooms of certain foreign students who had not been attending classes. The mayor chose to view this act as an infringement of his legal authority, and sued the rector.

The municipality also consolidated its authority by its policy of awarding scholarships to poor students and distributing grants to teachers at times of particular hardship or even in recognition of exceptional achievements. It also gave financial aid to the brighter students who went on to the Paris university, this being considered "a very great honor for the town." It gave funds to enable the new bachelors to celebrate their graduation appropriately. It was not indifferent to the personal safety of the students, as is revealed by an entry in the municipal archives for March 15, 1417: wooden gates were installed in the street on either side of the main entrance to the school in order to prevent people on horseback from galloping down it. However, it also assumed rights of censorship over the teaching: one schoolmaster, Jean Poucet, was made to stand on a scaffold and see his books committed to the flames "for having made wrong use of them."

In addition to his administrative duties, the rector was responsible for organizing the program of studies and for keeping an inventory of the books, of which he had to submit a copy to the choirmaster of Langres. He had to make sure that religious ceremonies were properly observed by the personnel and students of the schools, and he had certain representational functions. He had as assistants a vice-rector and the gatekeeper (*janitor seu portuarius*), the latter being charged with maintaining discipline in the school and empowered to administer corporal punishment when necessary. He also had to see to it that the school was provided with candles and that the books were properly stored and cared for. On occasion, he assumed the role of mediator in disputes between the students.

Music was taught daily by a *maître de chant* ("singing master") who led the choirs at solemn religious services. However, the principal center for the teaching of music was the ducal chapel. In 1424, Philip the Good provided funds for the assignment to the chapel of "four little children, innocent and of good behavior" to help in serving mass, and of a master for them who must be "sufficiently expert and of honest life" to teach them the sound doctrine and art of music in song, counterpoint, and descant.

The rector of the schools both taught and supervised the teaching in the boys' and girls' schools. His special fields were philosophy and mathematics. He was responsible for holding quarterly examinations and for organizing the *disputes solennelles* (as formal debates were called) held at the end of every leave period, at which all students of lower academic standing in the schools had to be present. For his pains, the rector, from 1415 onward, received six pennies a year from each male pupil and four pennies from each female, plus a few supplementary benefits and grants. The students and their teachers seem to have lived in an unexpectedly informal and democratic relationship, eating at the same table and calling each other *camarade*. On the day of the feast of Saint Nicolas, the patron saint of school boys, a great procession, called a *chevaulchée* ("cavalcade"), was held by the rectors, regents, teachers, and pupils of the schools of Dijon. When the duke made his solemn entry into his capital, he was greeted by the students shouting "Noël" and holding leafy branches.

Otherwise they behaved much as students always have and still do today: they indulged in rowdiness, destructiveness, and practical jokes at night in the streets of Dijon. Certain customs and sports were introduced into the duchy from the northern territories; cockfighting, for example, which was particularly popular among the students in Beaune.

It can be seen from the foregoing that the academic level at Dijon was modest compared with that of the great universities of the period.

While Dijon occupied a special position among the residences of the dukes, it was by no means the only one. Apart from the Hôtel d'Artois in Paris, the dukes took up residence in other parts of their possessions, and inclined to spend progressively less time in the duchy of Burgundy. Among the castles where they liked to stay, one stands out as a center both of entertainment and of artistic activity, that of Hesdin, in the county of Artois. Within the vast walled park, but distinct from the military fortifications of the castle, stood an extraordinary establishment known as the Château de Plaisance. It contained all kinds of ingenious and fantastic mechanical gadgets and devices designed to enchant and startle the visitor. This was no Burgundian creation although it is closely associated with the memory of the Valois dukes. The founder was Robert II, count of Artois in the late thirteenth century. He had lived several years as regent in Sicily, where many Arab scholars and scientists resided, and it seems likely that his source of inspiration was the Near East. Arab poets sang the praises of immense enclosed parks in the surroundings of Palermo; and an Arab manuscript of the early fourteenth century treats and illustrates the topic of hydraulic automatons, ingenious figures in human or animal form in which water pressure created movements which gave the illusion of life. Human figures would be seen walking, or discoursing with animated movements of arms and heads; wild beasts would be seen stalking their quarry; a lion would roar; and birds would sing in artificial trees.

However, the tradition of marvels of engineering in palaces goes back much further: in the first half of the ninth century the Byzantine emperor Theophilus had in his palace at Constantinople trees of gilded bronze in whose branches birds sang, while golden lions roared and flailed the ground with their tails, in addition to other astonishing things. The amusements at Hesdin were less refined and more robust than these. They were in keeping with the fondness for practical jokes and startling effects which we associate with the age and, in particular, the Burgundian court. At the entrance of the gallery which contained the mechanical surprises was one which wetted ladies from below when they stepped on it. Then there was a trick mirror which, when you tripped a lever, swung into your face and showered those under it with black or white dust. There was also a fountain "whose water flows when one wants it to, and always withdraws again to the spot whence it comes." Elsewhere a "hermit" appeared who caused rain to fall as though from heaven, accompanied by thunder, lightning, and snow "as is to be seen in the sky."

When Philip the Bold inherited Hesdin from his father-in-law in 1384, he kept up and enlarged the installations of his predecessors. In 1430, his grandson Philip the Good instructed his official painter, Colard le Voleur, to paint the gallery and to restore it to its original condition. The area containing gadgetry was doubled in size, and additional delights were provided for guests, such as a bridge which, when stepped upon, precipitated its victims into the water.

The duke loved to show off his toys; in 1462, the recently crowned king of France, Louis XI, was entertained there, and one must assume that care was taken to prevent him from taking a false step. In 1464, the queen of France was present there in honor of the visit by an English ambassadorial delegation. However, Hesdin was not only an amusement park. It was also an artistic center where orders given by the duke were carried out. Jean Miélot and Loyset Liédet, whose names are closely associated with the production and illumination of manuscripts for the ducal library, worked there, and the reputed writer and scribe David Aubert was born there. Unhappily, like all the palaces of the dukes, with the exception of what has survived at Dijon, nothing remains of Hesdin today: it was destroyed during the wars between Charles V and France in the following century.

CHAPTER III

Court Ceremonial and Fashions

URING the long siege by Charles the Bold of the town of Neuss on the Rhine in 1474–75, the chronicler Olivier de la Marche wrote a detailed account of the organization and functions of the ducal household. He first describes the duke's personal *chambre* ("staff") and then turns to what he calls the four *estates*, or supporting services of the establishment, ending with a detailed account of the duke's armed forces.

Though born in Dijon, Charles never resided there. In fact he only went back there again twice in his life. We must therefore assume that while the structure and functions of the court as described by La Marche remained pretty much the same wherever the duke might be residing, the number of officials must have varied substantially from place to place according to local conditions. La Marche states himself that he is drawing on thirty years of experience at court, and the account he gives may be taken as a composite image of the Valois court, whether at Dijon or at Brussels, Ghent, or Bruges.

The personnel of the duke's chapel numbered forty, including a bishop, a confessor, choristers, organists, and attendants in charge of the vestments, plate, and other church furniture. Mass and vespers were celebrated daily in the duke's presence, if it was possible for him to attend. Also on his household staff were an almoner and his assistant, who distributed substantial sums of money yearly in the duke's name to the sick and the indigent, including poor prisoners, spinsters, people whose homes had burned down, and bankrupt tradesmen. The almoner said grace at the duke's table.

Immediately after the chapel in importance came the ducal council and court "because, after divine service in church, justice is the second service which must be rendered to God." The council, with a permanent staff of officials such as magistrates, secretaries, and ushers, was usually presided over by the Chancellor of Burgundy, who was responsible both for discharging the council's own business and for the rendering of justice. In his absence, a bishop presided. Sessions of the council were frequently attended by the duke. The power of the chancellor exceeded even that of the Constable of France (who had a corresponding function), for the former had competence in all fields pertaining to the government of the duke's possessions, including finance, which was not within the constable's domain.

Charles, unlike his father, personally presided over public sessions twice a week in order to hear the claims and petitions "chiefly of the poor and the humble" who might complain of wrongs done them by the rich and the powerful, and who otherwise "could not approach him or come before his presence." These sessions took place on Mondays and Fridays. After his meal the duke went to the audience chamber which was close by, accompanied by the highest personnel of his household, "and no one would dare not to be present," adds the author. The duke sat on a richly decorated throne gleaming with cloth of gold, his feet resting on a wide stool, with three steps covered with tapestry. Below him was a little bench on which two magistrates and an auditor kneeled when reading out cases. Nearby a secretary, also on his knees, recorded the proceedings, which he then passed on to a clerk who strung each succeeding document with the others on a long ribbon. Behind these officials were seated in appropriate order various princes, ambassadors, knights of the Golden Fleece and other dignitaries. Behind the duke's throne stood those squires whose office pertained to his personal service, "excluding the Master of the Horse, because the functions of this office were discharged publicly." The duke also had a provost, with men-at-arms under his orders whose function it was to prosecute criminal cases in peacetime. His authority extended to all territories under the duke's jurisdiction with the exception of those belonging to members of the duke's own household, for which the various masters of the household were directly responsible to the duke. In time of war, the provost was responsible, under the duke's authority, for all legal matters and for the administration of justice among the armed forces. He was empowered to hear all cases except those arising from an act of war.

Next in order of importance, after religious obligations and the dispensing of justice, came matters relating to war which, we are told, is sometimes necessary in order that the rights of the ruler may be protected and his authority upheld, and through which God can and must be served, by waging war in a just cause and in due form. For the consideration of military questions, the duke had a committee of military advisers consisting of four knights who, with the assistance of a restricted number of the highest officials of the court, made their recommendations to him. And since the settlement of weighty problems requires financial support, the fourth way of serving God (after divine service, justice, and war) is that of finance. In a thinly veiled criticism of Philip the Good, the point is made that the prince who keeps his eye on these matters serves both God and himself in profit and in conscience, whereas the one who spends money without knowing where it is going nor whence it comes encourages those under him to feather their own nests and to waste money, thereby causing great damage to his people. Hence the importance of the *chambre des finances* which kept account of all receipts and expenditures both in the public domain and in the duke's personal establishment. Charles the Bold paid strict attention to financial matters: "He comes very often in person, and no accounts are certified without him, or without his personal seal being affixed to them. He signs all expenditures with his own hand and knows exactly what cash he has in hand and how much he spends." All accounts went through him, and he liked to sit in the midst of his financial staff balancing his receipts and expenditures, "the only difference between them being that the duke makes calculations with chips of gold and the others with chips of silver."

Within the duke's household lived a number of *grands pensionnaires* whom he personally supported financially: six dukes and twelve princes, counts, and marquises. Beside these were many others more or less dependent on him, in addition to a considerable number of knights on the payroll.

The chamberlain had the key of, and access to, the duke's rooms and was the keeper of the seal. He carried the duke's banner in battle and received in his name the oaths of vassals. His room was next to that of the duke, at whose table he ate. Another important official was the grand master of the household, who had the privilege of attending sessions of all councils dealing with both justice and war. He received visiting princes and embassies. He served the duke at table in person at the four major religious feasts and on state occasions, when he entered the room preceding the dish destined for the duke, carrying a baton raised on high. However it was not he who first tasted the dish as a precaution against any attempt to poison the duke. This privilege—if it may be called one—was reserved for his immediate subordinate, the first master of the household, or, in his absence, one of his colleagues. Once the dish had been set before the duke, the grand master of the household was in charge of all procedures relating to the serving of the meal.

The foregoing rights and privileges were inherent in the office of grand master of the household resident in the ducal palace at Dijon. However, in other parts of the ducal territories they were personally delegated by the duke at his pleasure. The first master and four assistants between them supervised the security police, intra-household personal relations, protocol, and ceremonies, and were responsible for a daily accounting of the duke's personal expenditures, including wages and the cost of the food of the household. The cleaning and upkeep of the duke's apartments were the responsibility of four *sommeliers*, "housekeepers" (the word only acquired its exclusive association with the cellar in later times, when restaurants became common), of whom the senior one had board and lodging in the palace, the three others only being entitled to board. These functionaries also had keys to the duke's rooms and personal access to him at all times.

For personal companionship the duke was attended by sixteen squires of noble birth who accompanied him wherever he went, on foot or on horseback, and who looked after his wardrobe and his personal needs. As an additional measure of security they slept close by his room. After the day's work was over, the duke would withdraw with his squires into his rooms, where they would entertain the duke, some with songs, others by reading to him, others by discussing feats of arms or of love "so as to make time pass for the duke in pleasant novelties." These squires also enjoyed the privilege of board and lodging in the palace.

The risk involved in being responsible for the health of the duke was spread among six doctors. They stood behind his chair while he sat at table, examined carefully what he was being given to eat and gave him advice on his diet. They naturally also had direct access to the duke and were fed, though not housed, at court. Four surgeons were available to the duke and members of his household, and "they are certainly not among those of the household who have least to do," we read, for the duke was so active militarily that there were often many who were suffering from wounds, "so that fifty surgeons would have had their hands full."

The duke's treasure was under the custody of a keeper and his assistant. As a personal staff the duke had some forty valets, some on a permanent, others on a rotating basis. The word *valet* should be understood in a different sense from the purely menial connotation it later acquired. A valet was someone appointed by the duke to discharge a specific function for him at his pleasure: barbers, cobblers, tailors, seamsters, furriers, and so forth. Artists were honored by being appointed *varletz de chambre* of the duke. The sculptor Claus Sluter, the painters Jan van Eyck and Jean Malouel, held this title, as well as the architects who built Champmol and enlarged the ducal palace. Then there were also those whose functions approximated those of the modern valet, who looked after the upkeep of the duke's rooms.

A keeper of the spices, assisted by two subordinates, was responsible for obtaining and looking after the medicines and drugs the duke might need, as well as the spices and sweetmeats of which he partook at table. An indication of how trusted the holders of this position were is that they had the privilege of giving the duke what he asked for in the way of medicines directly, without having to go through anyone else. Obviously the possibilities for an attempt on the duke's life would here be particularly great.

The foregoing functions, and staff amounting to at least five hundred people, comprised the duke's household or *chambre*. In addition to these must be numbered four officials, each with a staff of about fifty, responsible for providing food, bread, and wine, for carving the meat and serving at table; and last but not least, the master of the horse. Of these four estates, that of the *panetier* was *primus inter pares* because of the symbolic association of his function with the consecrated bread of the mass. Together with the chamberlain, he served the duke at table in person on the four major religious feast days. At other times he designated the member of his staff who should represent him. The service itself was an elaborate ritual which included applying to the dish served to the duke the test of the "unicorn's horn" (narwhal's tusk) believed to have the property of revealing the presence of poison, and the observance of such details as the way in which the salt cellar should be held: "Between the fingers at a spot between the feet and the bowl . . . this being different from the goblet which must be held by its foot," etc. The members of the serving staff were all drawn from noble families. The duke promoted his pages to the position of *varletz servans,* thus opening the way to them of rising to the rank of squire *pour la bouche* and on to higher positions "according to their qualities and to the rank of the house from which they come."

The next function in seniority to that of *panetier* was that of *eschanson* ("purveyor of wine") since wine, like bread, had the symbolic dignity of participation in the mystery of the Communion; "and it is very right that the services of bread and wine should have first place." Our chronicler is greatly puzzled by the word *eschanson*, which seemed to be in no way related to the words *vine* or *wine* (it is in fact derived through Spanish and Portuguese from the old German word meaning to pour: in modern German, *schenken*), whereas the word *panetier* came from the word for bread, while the function of the carver was implicit in his title of *escuier trenchant*. He speculates that since the prince eats in public and is observed by all present, and since he must be a mirror of all virtues and propriety, and since "wine carries in itself more [cause for] greediness than any dish served, and it would not be seemly to call out frequently for more wine for the prince," it had been decided by the wise men of old that a word unrelated to wine should be devised for this function. Carried away by his fancy, our friend suggests that *eschanson* is "a gay name deliberately coined from the word for song because our forefathers and their guests were stimulated and made gay by wine, and the first and principal way of expressing gaiety is by song."

That this section of the ducal household was kept busy is revealed by the statement that no year went by in which the court of Burgundy did not account for the consumption of more than one thousand *queues de vin* (the *queue* or barrel of Beaune wine contained 458 liters, so that this figure represents a minimum consumption of 458,000 liters, about 120,000 gallons, yearly), "and in some years one thousand more, according to the number of gatherings and festivities." The ritual of serving the wine was as complicated as that of serving the rest of the meal. Since it is even simpler to administer poison through drink than through food, the duke's silver cup also had a length of "unicorn's horn" attached to it by a chain wherewith to test the wine. In order to spare the duke the embarrassment of having to call publicly for more wine, the *eschanson* stood in front of him, watching alertly for a sign from the prince when he wished to be served.

Next in order of precedence was the *escuier trenchant* ("carving squire"), who outranked the master of the stable because he was in charge of the duke's pennant in battle, his responsibility being to stay close to the duke throughout the action so that all might see where the duke was. Had it not been for the special considerations which determined the rank of the *panetier* and of the *eschanson*, he would have had precedence over them because he was closer to the duke for the satisfaction of his physical needs. When the duke wished to eat in private, it was he who assumed the functions of the other two. Being familiar with the duke's tastes and preferences, he was on terms of greater intimacy with him. Like his colleagues he had a staff of fifty, and with them he served in person on the four major religious feast days, participating in the ritual of testing the duke's food and wine. He was responsible for, but had no authority in, the kitchen. He could make his views on the cooking or the presentation of the food known to the master of the household who would then take the matter up with the cook.

The kitchen was run by two *escuiers de cuisine* (kitchen squires) who had authority over the staff. They were also responsible for obtaining the meat and fish and for settling the terms of the purchases involved under a yearly contract. The cook personally selected the choicest meat and fish for the duke's table, the rest going to those who boarded at the duke's expense. The *escuiers de cuisine* had a right to the hides of prize animals offered to the duke as gifts, whereas the cook could keep their fat for himself, to be sold profitably to chandlers. The *escuier de cuisine* on duty carried a lighted torch behind the meat when it was brought into the duke's presence. Before it went the usher of the dining room also carrying a torch—a further example of the precautions taken against possible sneak attempts on the duke's life.

The duke had three cooks, each of whom, it seems, was on duty for a period of four months in the year. In his kitchen, the cook's authority was supreme: he "must command, give orders, and be obeyed." His command post was a tall chair strategically placed between the serving table and the chimney, so that he could see and control all that was going on. He held in his hand a long-handled wooden ladle with a dual function: first, to enable him to taste the soup and the sauce and, second, to chase unauthorized children out of the kitchen and, when necessary, to chastise workers who were not doing their job properly. The cook was personally responsible for the contents and the security of the spice cabinet. On being informed that the duke wished to eat, he changed into clean clothes and had the saucemaker put a clean cloth on the serving table. He then hung a napkin over his right shoulder and proceeded to sample the dish about to be served to the duke, both for taste and for wholesomeness. He had the privilege on certain special occasions of presenting a dish to the duke in person, of carrying out the test himself, and of taking a drink from the sideboard. This occurred when the first truffles and the first fresh herrings of the year were presented to the duke. The technique of packing herring in salt in small casks—thus keeping them sweet and fresh for some time—had been developed in the Low Countries in the early fifteenth century. Philip the Good became count of Holland in 1433, and the custom of rushing the year's first catch of herring to its ruler has survived to this day. Each year it is offered ceremoniously to the queen of the Netherlands. As for the truffles, they were indigenous to the duchy, though conceded to be of inferior quality to those of the Périgord.

A new cook was picked "by solemn election" from among the *escuiers de cuisine*. These then individually informed the masters of the household of their candidate, who was formally appointed by the duke. La Marche emphasizes the importance and responsibility of what he calls this "subtle and sumptuous profession." Should the cook be absent or sick, it was up to the masters of the household to pick a temporary substitute, probably the roaster or soupmaker most familiar with the duke's tastes. The kitchen staff numbered twenty-five, each one charged with a particular task. It also included several scullions who served as unpaid apprentices to pluck the fowl, clean the fish, and do other menial chores. Together with the *galopins* or *happe-lopins* (errand boys, the lowest in the kitchen hierarchy), they kept the vast spits turning over the fires.

In addition to the roaster and soupmaker, there were two saucemakers. Although the fruiterer was not strictly speaking a member of the kitchen staff, he is mentioned here because his function was related to the duke's table. He was responsible for supplying not only fruit but also the all-important commodity of wax for the tremendous quantity of candles and torches needed for the illumination of the palace and for religious festivals. And why should it be the fruiterer who was responsible for the supply of wax? "It is indeed because wax is made by bees from the flowers from which comes the fruit; this is why this matter has been very properly settled." The fruiterer had a permanent staff of eight and could call on additional help for carrying torches to light the duke's way when he went out at night. As an example of the meticulous care with which accounts were kept, a special mark was stamped onto the base of the small torches used to precede and to follow the dishes brought to the duke's table. In order to get a new one, the stump with the mark on it had first to be handed in.

The "fourth estate" (in the context of fifteenth-century

Burgundy), was the master of the horse, who, La Marche points out, should be called and referred to only as *escuier* and not *escuier d'escuyrie*, because the stable is already implicit in the word *escuier*. Unable to resist a joke, he adds that "there is no estate in the household which may be called 'Escuier' without a tail, other than that of Master of the Horse." The *escuier* also had fifty men under him and was expected to combine the qualities of physical strength, valor, wisdom, and resourcefulness: strength because in battle he carried the duke's standard (not to be confused with the lighter pennant) which was large and heavy and raised on high above all others; valor, because he had to give full support to the duke and rally all around him; wisdom and resourcefulness, because he concerned himself with all the ceremonies organized in honor of the duke and their decoration. He also armed and equipped the duke for both war and tourneys or jousts. In wartime his room was closest to that of the duke; in peacetime it was the farthest away. He held the ceremonial sword before the duke on all official occasions, whether on foot or on horseback, with the blade resting on his right shoulder. He had under his care the duke's trumpeters and other musicians. When the duke jousted, the *escuier* was each time entitled to keep for himself the decorations and trappings worn by the duke and his horse, save those of gold or precious stones.

To the foregoing personnel must be added heralds, pursuivants, kings-of-arms, and a numerous personal bodyguard of archers, on foot and mounted, not to mention the armed forces of infantry, artillery, and cavalry with their supporting elements. It is not surprising that contemporaries were awed by such a scale of living and accorded to the duke of Burgundy a degree of deference second to none.

The minutely regulated sequence of actions and motions

observed on all occasions involving the presence and the service of the duke and members of his family evokes an elaborate choreography. This emphasis on ceremonial did not, however, originate with the court of Burgundy. It had been developed over the centuries at the court of France, and taken over by the dukes as princes of the royal blood. It was strictly applied in keeping with their dignity and with an eye to the impression of wealth and power which it was in their interest to create.

An account has fortunately come down to us of the procedures and the rationale of protocol governing the conduct of, and relations between, members of various levels of the social hierarchy in the fifteenth century. It was written by Eleanor of Poitiers whose mother, Isabel of Sousa, was Portuguese and had accompanied Isabel of Portugal to Burgundy in 1429 for her marriage with Philip the Good early in the following year. She wrote it toward the end of her life in the last quarter of the century, by which time, greatly to her distress and disapproval, ceremonial traditions were becoming increasingly modified and neglected: "Mention shall not be made," she writes, "of those men or women who assert that these things were done in those times and that the present time is another world; such allegations do not suffice to abolish ancient and established customs, and no attention should be paid to them because these things must not happen." It is not only in our own age that we hear the voice of King Canute! She describes meticulously both the rules of precedence and what is fitting for people to wear according to their station in life, as well as the problems raised when one party insists on deferring to the other against the rules.

The example she gives of this occurred in 1456 when the dauphin (later Louis XI), having quarreled with his father, sought refuge without warning at the court of Philip the

Good, who was then residing in Brussels. The duke himself was absent at the time, and so the dauphin was received by the duchess Isabel and her daughter-in-law, the countess of Charolais, who was expecting a child, the future Mary of Burgundy. As soon as the ladies heard that the dauphin was arriving, they went forth to greet him. He dismounted, kissed the duchess, her daughter-in-law, and the other ladies present. "After this he took the duchess by the arm and sought to give her precedence before him, which she would never have taken on her own. However, he insisted so much that she said to him: 'Sir, it seems to me that you wish people to make fun of me, for you want me to do something which it is not right for me to do.' " The dauphin protested that this was not the case and that it was proper for him to give her precedence, for he was the most miserable man of the kingdom of France and did not know where he could seek refuge save with his "*Bel Oncle*" the duke of Burgundy, and her. "They continued discussing the problem for over a quarter of an hour, and finally, when he realized that Madame would not go first for anything in the world, he gave her his left hand and took her with him, at which said lady protested vigorously, for she did not wish to go hand in hand with him, and said that she should not do it; but he wanted her to do it, and because of this she did it; and thus it was that Madame led him to his room, and when she left him she knelt on the ground."

There is a twofold explanation for all this embarrassment on the part of the duchess: first, by common consent, the king of France and all his children outranked all other princes. The scale of hierarchy descended from them in accordance with the degree of proximity in relationship to the king. Even the duke of Burgundy felt constrained to kneel before a royal prince, not to mention the king of France himself. Thus for the dauphin to try to make the duchess take precedence over him amounted to an attempt to put her in a false position. Second, the dauphin's subsequent action in placing her on a par with him by taking her by her right hand (a degree higher than if he had taken her left hand with his right hand) was merely another way of demeaning himself and thus of putting her in the position of infringing the rules of protocol, which was considered to be both ludicrous and personally humiliating.

When the duke returned to Brussels, the duchess and their daughter-in-law hastened to the courtyard of the palace to await his arrival. When the dauphin heard this, he rushed out of his room and joined the ladies, much to their discomfiture. The duchess begged him to go in again, saying that it was improper for him to come forward to greet the duke, but he refused to oblige her. It was now the duke's turn to be embarrassed by the dauphin: "When the duke learned that the dauphin was waiting for him in the middle of the courtyard, he dismounted at the gate and as soon as he caught sight of the dauphin, he knelt down on the ground. The dauphin started forward, but the duchess, whom he was holding by the arm, restrained him; and the duke moved forward and rendered a second obeisance before the dauphin was able to move toward him: and when he did come up to him, the duke knelt on the ground and the dauphin seized him by the arms and they walked to the steps in this way with their arms round each other; and thence the duke led him to his room, there taking leave of him and went into his own room and the ladies to theirs." This display of excessive and embarrassing humility by the dauphin is consistent with the character and the methods of operation of the future Louis XI.

It was not only in personal comportment and in the

observance of established procedures that niceties of social hierarchy found expression. There were equally strict rules for the decoration of rooms for certain occasions. These extended even to the quality and the color of the fabrics, the kinds of furniture and how it should be arranged in a room, in keeping with the station of the individuals involved.

When Mary of Burgundy was born, her mother occupied one of two large beds, four or five feet apart from each other. Between the heads of the beds was a chair with a high back "like those big chairs of former times." Before the fireplace stood a small bed mounted on rollers. A large awning of green damask stretched above both beds and curtains of green satin hung around them, only leaving open the space between them. The fringes of the awning were of green silk. Access to the two beds could be closed off by drawing a curtain which hung on rings two or three feet in front of the foot of the two beds. Between them was a similar curtain which was never drawn, rolled up high and wedged up behind the back of the chair. The little bed was surmounted by a pyramid-shaped green damask awning of the same size as the bed, with green satin curtains hanging from it. The whole room was lined with green silk and the floor was covered with deep pile rugs. The two large beds and the little bed had ermine covers lined with fine purple cloth which extended beyond the edges of the fur itself, so that when they were stretched on the beds, the cloth hung down to the floor. On top of these lay two cloths of fine gauze. The chair between the two large beds was upholstered in cloth of gold shot with crimson. In the same room stood a large sideboard with four broad shelves covered with white linen cloths, on which were arrayed crystal vases and dishes set with gold and precious stones, brought out only for such occasions. Among these were three golden bowls for sweetmeats, of which two were valued at thirty and forty thousand crowns. Above the side-board was stretched a panel of cloth of gold shot with crimson, with a black velvet border on which was embroidered in fine gold the device of Philip the Good: a steel striking sparks from flint. This scene of splendor was illuminated by two silver candlesticks. Nearby, on a low table stood pots and cups in which to serve drinks to callers after they had taken sweetmeats.

From the moment of her birth, Mary of Burgundy was engulfed in the ceremonial obligatory for one of her station: she too slept in a room with two large beds in it. Her cradle stood before the fireplace, but her room had no little bed on rollers in it, as did her mother's. The two beds were covered in green and purple damask, the curtains being of the same color; there were no curtains across the ends of the beds or between them. An awning of green and purple damask stretched over the cradle which had a floor-length cover of ermine skins. The floor had deep pile rugs on it as in the other room.

There was also a large anteroom in which callers waited to be received. It contained a large bed covered in crimson satin, with an awning and a bedspread of the same material. On each of these was embroidered a sunburst covering the entire surface, said to have been presented to the duke by the town of Utrecht (where one of his bastards had recently been installed as bishop and from which that particular room took its name). A sideboard with three shelves and numerous, though less precious, dishes and vases stood at the far end of the room from the bed, at whose head stood a little velvet-covered chair "like those on which princesses often sit"; and on its seat was a square piece of cloth of gold.

The exact description of each piece of furniture and object, of the color and texture and of the position of each in relation to everything else within the room creates a sense of spatial unity, almost of physical participation akin to that which we feel when we lose ourselves in the contemplation of the individual elements of a scene in a painting of the period. A sense of freshness of experience telescopes the centuries magically, so that we seem to hear the crackle of the fire in the great fireplace, catch the flicker of shadows across the walls and ceiling, the play of light on embroideries and cloth of gold; and we almost hear the footfall of someone about to enter the room.

Until the fourteenth century, women wore long gowns with little variety of style or decoration. Men for their part were chiefly concerned with the requirements of physical protection in the form of armor and coats of mail. The evolution and emancipation of social organization introduced a corresponding increase in variety of dress. The trend originated at the French court, and was encouraged by such wealthy and cultivated patrons as the dukes of Berry, Anjou, and Burgundy in the period with which we are concerned. It culminated in an eye-catching display of the richest fabrics, the brightest colors, the most fanciful headdresses, and the most exotic articles of personal adornment. The contributions to taste and fashion of France and of the Low Countries merged at the court of Burgundy, whose first duke struck at once the note of almost outrageous luxury and ostentation which has since been considered typical of his dynasty.

In 1389, Queen Isabeau of Bavaria, the wife of King Charles VI, made her first entry into Paris. For this occasion Philip the Bold took with him four velvet coats set with pearls, gold flowers, and jewels. He wore a scarlet doublet on which were embroidered forty lambs and swans in pearls. From the necks of the lambs and the swans hung little gold bells. Oak leaves were embroidered on a green coat, and its sleeves were decorated with twigs of hawthorn between which lambs, also made up of pearls, sported. On another occasion Philip the Bold appeared in a flowing black cloak reaching to the ground. On its left sleeve glowed a spray of gold roses set with twenty-two flowers consisting of sapphires, rubies, and pearls. He also had with him a short cherry-red velvet doublet, on which were embroidered polar bears with gold collars and muzzles set with precious stones. When his daughter Margaret was married, her gown was decorated with over one hundred pearls. To his future daughter-in-law he sent three different lengths of brocade, some costly white satin for her wedding gown, and a reddish patterned silk for a four-piece evening dress. He included also some crimson velvet, some cloth for a simpler dress, and cloth of gold from Lucca to make a hanging for the wedding ceremony. In addition to the members of the ducal family, princes of the church were often recipients of rich presents of cloth from the duke; the bishop of Chalon received fine Brussels cloth for a coat and 1,250 squirrel skins with which to line it.

It had long been the tradition that every year on the day of the Feast of the Holy Cross the count of Flanders should offer new festive robes to the statue of the Virgin in the Cathedral of Tournai. When Philip the Bold succeeded his father-in-law as count, he did not fail to respect this tradition. His son, John the Fearless, had two fur-lined brocaded dresses made for it. In turn, Philip the Good ordered enough cloth of gold from Giovanni Arnolfini of Lucca in 1424 to make robes for both the Virgin of Tournai and another statue venerated in the region.

Thanks to paintings and miniatures from illuminated manuscripts as well as tapestries which have come down to us from this period, we can form a clear idea not only of the style of fashions but of colors popular in court circles. The prevalent passion for investing visual objects with a symbolic meaning extended to colors. Philip the Good preferred to dress in black. René of Anjou liked to vary black with white and gray. In garments worn at festivities, violent contrasts of vivid colors predominated, whereas in everyday life quieter shades such as gray and violet were popular, as well as white and black. Yellow and brown are seldom seen, the former, when blatantly displayed in certain contexts, being tantamount to a declaration of hostility. Blue and green are relatively rare, being associated with love and the complications arising from it: blue, while signifying fidelity, came to be an object of ridicule in dress as being tantamount to a confession of infidelity. A woman wearing a blue undercoat was mocked as being deceived by her husband. A long blue gown could be taken as signifying that she was an adulteress. In France, a blue jacket marked the wearer as a cuckold, and blue was also generally associated with fools. Green was suggestive of a declaration of passionate love, and could thus only be worn with discretion.

Perhaps the boldest flights of the imagination went to headgear, especially for ladies. Men, who long continued to wear the medieval cowl with streamers falling over the shoulders, also turned to fancy hats and caps. Hats of Lombardy straw were worn in the summer and felt hats in winter, as well as beaver-skin hats from Germany. Headgear became a precarious repository for gold ornaments and jewels, sometimes of inestimable value. One peacock feather made up of pearls and rubies which Philip the Good wore in his hat in 1420 was valued at fifty thousand crowns. Charles the Bold loved to wear the state jewels on his head even during military campaigns: in the booty captured by the Swiss after their victory at Grandson in 1476 was a yellow velvet hat decorated with a gold crown and large pearls, sapphires, and rubies, a pearl chain with six strands, and a white and red ostrich feather.

A fashion of ladies' headwear that was very popular was the hennin, a long, tapering cone of fine fabrics, from which hung veils, and which came to be known as the "steeple head-dress." Even its length was determined by the social standing of the wearer: while a princess might have one a yard long, two feet only were deemed permissible for ladies of the nobility. Thus social status could be identified at a glance. "No one," wrote that arbiter of manners, Eleanor of Poitiers, "must be permitted to exhibit greater presumption or cere-moniousness than is appropriate to that person's station and than have traditionally been the custom and usage." Horned headdresses as well as other bizarre shapes were also in vogue. Isabel of Portugal brought some exotic touches of fashion to the Burgundian court. When the duke's ambassadors arrived at Lisbon in 1429 with Jan van Eyck (who painted a portrait of Isabel for Philip the Good), she wore a cloak slit on both sides, and such a strange turbanlike headdress of blue velvet that the Burgundians at first took her for a knight. This account makes us regret all the more that van Eyck's painting has not survived.

All this extravagance and display drew scorn and criticism from moralists, who railed against the billowing coifs which they compared with sailing ships and against other fanciful forms which led them to upbraid women "who could not be content with two horns like animals, but insisted on wearing no less than eight, to which they even fastened bells." Men were just as reprehensible, with their tight waists and short tunics and their shoes in the Polish style with long toes tapering and curving to a point several inches long. Mention is made of a pair of shoes with points some two feet long, which had to be secured by golden chains fastened to the wearer's knees.

That all this sartorial eccentricity was generally resented by the common people as provocative is revealed by the enthusiastic popular response to invectives launched against it by one Friar Thomas, a Carmelite preacher from Brittany. He traveled on a small mule through parts of northern France and the Low Countries delivering fiery sermons to the population. He liked to denounce the sins and the immorality of the clergy, but he took especial joy in fulminating against the luxury of female apparel. "He was," we read in an old translation of a contemporary chronicle, "so vehement against them that no woman thus dressed dared to appear in his presence, for he was accustomed, when he saw any of them with such dresses, to excite the little boys to torment and plague them, giving them certain days of pardon for doing so, and which he said he had the power of granting. He ordered the boys to shout after them, 'Au hennin! au hennin!' even when the ladies were departed from him and from hearing his invectives; and the boys pursuing them endeavored to pull down these monstrous headdresses, so that the ladies were forced to seek shelter in places of safety." Friar Thomas succeeded—out of a sense of self-protection on the part of his victims—in bringing about a certain reform in fashions, but not for long "for like as snails, when any one passes by them, draw in their horns, and when all danger seems over, put them forth again, so these ladies, shortly after the preacher had quitted their country, forgetful of his doctrine and abuse, began to resume their former colossal headdresses, and wore them even higher than before."

In the center of the display of sartorial fireworks stood the sober figure of Philip the Good, who, as already mentioned, preferred to wear black in deference, it has been alleged, to the memory of his murdered father. He may also have been conscious of the fact that black silks and velvets showed off to their best advantage the sumptuous jewels he liked to wear. When in 1461 he accompanied the dauphin to Paris for his coronation as Louis XI, his cap and cloak and the trappings of his horse glittered with precious stones, in striking contrast to the simplicity, indeed the drabness, of the dauphin's apparel. This implicit arrogance and condescending attitude by the duke of Burgundy toward the man who was about to become his liege lord as king of France was not lost on contemporaries, least of all, we may be sure, on Louis himself.

Among the most magnificent and colorful ceremonies recorded were those which took place in 1468 on the occasion of the marriage of Charles the Bold to Margaret of York in Bruges. The streets were hung with tapestries and all kinds of decorations. Scenes from the Bible and from mythology were enacted on specially erected stages. Margaret of York, in a red litter escorted by knights of the Golden Fleece, wore a white gown lined with cloth of gold. Her retinue of Scottish ladies followed, mounted on white steeds. The representatives of nations with financial and commercial offices in Bruges marched in procession. At their head were the Venetians in red, followed by the Florentines in blue and black, the Spaniards in violet, the Genoese also in violet, and the merchants of the Hanseatic league in lilac cloth lined with fur. Brightly dressed pages headed each delegation, the Florentines wearing silver cloth jackets under short capes of red velvet and mounted on horses with blankets trimmed with blue velvet. It would be repetitious to pursue the interminable description of the clothes and jewels worn at the banquets and tournaments which followed.

In contrast to his father, Charles the Bold was a man of personal austerity, who shunned the flippant gaiety of court entertainment. However, he too recognized the political influence of displays of wealth. When he went to Trier in 1473 in the vain expectation of wresting a royal crown from the emperor Frederick III, he fairly dripped with pearls and precious stones, outshining the emperor much as his father had outshone Louis XI a dozen years earlier—with equally negative results. When a thunderstorm broke over his head, Charles preferred to get soaked rather than dim his radiance by putting on a cloak.

"In all this splendor," writes the historian H. Wescher, "apart from naïve childishness, there was already an almost unhealthy mania for extravagance, which hinted at the impending decline of this period." Such judgments, which have been so often passed as to have become commonplace, are questionable. They convey a smug note of nineteenth-century moralizing, with the implication of pride running before a fall; but a historical and cultural study of the period to which they refer fails to establish their relevance to the course of events or to the evolution of society. The political role of manifestations of splendor has already been stressed. The enjoyment of luxury is a universal human characteristic, failing which it would not have been politically effective; and it has been catered to by those in power in all lands throughout history. To call it "naïve childishness" may be morally satisfying, but such a charge cannot be brought exclusively, or even peculiarly, to the Burgundian court. To refer to an "almost unhealthy mania" is to introduce a new or at least an additional explanation for what is called "the impending decline of this period."

In fact, the period under consideration was one of transition from the medieval world to that of humanism. Traditional institutions and forms of thought were losing their hold on men's minds precisely because new horizons of human experience were emerging. Erasmus was born during the lifetime of Charles the Bold. The distinctive attitudes and interests of Renaissance man were emerging in northern Europe coincidentally with Italy, though more laboriously, as European society gradually freed itself from the restrictive political, social, and economic traditions of the institutions and ideals of feudalism and chivalry. These were being loosened from within by forces of growth for which there was no precedent and the implications of which contemporaries could not yet understand. Rather than see this period as one of decline, it seems historically more accurate to see it as one of flowering in the arts, of the dawn of intellectual emancipation, and as a bridge between the Middle Ages and the foundations of the modern world.

In this respect, Isabel of Portugal played an important role. She encouraged and protected scholars and translators in the fields of classical history and literature. Thanks to her patronage, Vasco de Lucena, a scholar from her native country who had studied in Paris, became a member of the court. Through his translations of the *History of Alexander*, by Quintus Curtius, and of Xenophon's *Cyropedia* for the ducal library, he undoubtedly exercised a considerable influence on the intellectual climate around him; and manuscripts of his works multiplied in the second half of the century. His approach to classical antiquity, based on respect for historical truth and rejection of myth and error, was in tune with the spirit of humanism south of the Alps.

It is perhaps permissible to suggest certain reasons for the extent to which the age of the Valois dukes has been vilified as politically irresponsible and socially degenerate. First of all, the political history of Burgundy under the four dukes was marked first by gradual, later by accelerating, withdrawal from the authority of the French monarchy, and by movement toward the goal of political independence. This occurred at a time when Europe was experiencing the early stages of its transformation into a pattern determined by nationalistic currents. Historically, the genius of Louis XI was correctly to sense in the House of Burgundy a dangerous threat to France's national interests and to spare no effort in contributing to the downfall of Charles the Bold. This lesson, taught to schoolboys over the generations, has moved French historians in particular to explain not only why the policy of the dukes failed, but why it was right and inevitable that it should fail. The latter urge encouraged the injection into the study of the period of a note of moral condemnation of Valois policy, rather along the lines of what one might have expected to read in books by British historians writing about the thirteen colonies if our struggle for independence had collapsed at Valley Forge. Nationalistic sentiment has encouraged later historians to censure the dukes for the violation of principles which were not of their age. This patriotic approach toward the history of Burgundy, which, it should be emphasized, has been largely abandoned by historians today, found it convenient to draw on the contemporary accounts of the chronicles to paint a picture of a society in decay, consumed by vanity, lust for power, and a morbid imagination, with an insatiable appetite for luxury and irresponsible self-indulgence—as though the events so fulsomely described by the ducal panegyrists constituted the daily life of the court. Hence the traditional picture over the centuries of a somewhat monstrous and reprehensible Burgundian experiment, spawned by the unnatural political ambition of the dukes and nurtured by the aberrations of a self-indulgent court. Even a historian and sociologist of the distinction of

J. Huizinga felt morally impelled to throw a few rocks at the Burgundian court, in particular for having indulged in tastes and pastimes which were merely those of the age in which it existed, and which stand out only because the dukes saw to it that they were more plentifully and minutely described than by any other court in Europe.

CHAPTER IV

The Dukes and the Arts

T HE name of Burgundy is traditionally associated with patronage of the arts on a grand scale. However, indulgence in vast expenditures on jewels, goldsmiths' work, tapestries, precious textiles, illuminated manuscripts, and costly articles of personal adornment was not peculiar to the dukes. They were neither breaking new ground nor launching tastes not already fully shared by the other princes of the royal house of France. The havoc and the misery which the Hundred Years' War brought to the people of France did not inhibit the privileged minority from acquiring rare and costly things.

This passion was personified in the sons of King John the Good, Charles V having been an avid collector of manuscripts. His library, housed in a tower of the palace of the Louvre, laid the basis for the Royal, later the National, Library. Furthermore, his taste encompassed all manner of objects of luxury, of which he had a great number. His brothers, the dukes John of Berry, Louis of Anjou, and Philip of Burgundy vied with each other in collecting the most precious and exotic works of art. Thus it was the royal court of France which set the tone and fashion for others to follow. If we should be tempted to condemn these princes and nobles for a lack of social conscience characteristic of the age in which they lived, we should also note that their predilection for objects of quality in all media acted as a powerful stimulus and incentive to artists and craftsmen in competition with each other for lucrative orders in a period of economic depression. There was a high premium on aesthetic innovation and imaginativeness as well as on technical virtuosity.

Every New Year's Day, the members of the royal family presented costly gifts to each other as well as to close friends, noblemen around them, and certain holders of high office. Thanks to the survival of many inventories of this period, we are well informed on these presents. They reflect an imaginative and fanciful taste, as may be seen from the following examples listed in the records for the year 1393: to his nephew, King Charles VI, the duke of Burgundy sent two clasps, one decorated with the royal arms and the other with a female figure seated in an orchard. The duke of Orléans (who was to be assassinated fourteen years later by the duke of Burgundy's son) received a clasp with a "feathered bird." Other clasps mentioned among the gifts for this year were decorated with "a white lion lying in a park" and "a white lady"; also "a lady in green seated within a white flower." The admiral of the French fleet was given a clasp with a white flower and two squirrels. We also read of a unicorn of white enamel and of a white hare with black spots. The partiality to the use of white enamel in the decoration of jewelry of this period reflects the influence of Italian taste and craftsmanship introduced north of the Alps by merchants and money lenders from Lombardy and Tuscany.

In addition to jewelry, gifts comprised precious cloth, gold and silver plate, bowls, vases, statuettes, tapestries, reliquaries, and precious stones. It was also permissible to offer oneself a present, part of which would be paid by an expected donor. One such example was a silver tabernacle containing a scene of the Annunciation wrought in enameled gold and studded with pearls, in which the duke of Burgundy had indulged himself. The cost of this bauble being a little steep even for the ducal pocket, he prevailed on the king to offer him as his

New Year's gift a sum of money large enough to enable him to pay the difference without wincing too much.

The prodigality of the dukes of Burgundy in distributing gifts served the same general purpose as ceremonial magnificence and sumptuous banquets. The wealth and treasure accumulated by Philip the Good subsequently earned him the reputation of having been a precursor of the Florentine Maecenas, Lorenzo de' Medici. "After his father's death," writes the chronicler Philippe de Commynes, "Charles [the Bold] was one of the richest and most awe-inspiring figures of Christendom; and he came into the possession of more jewelry, tapestries, books, and textiles than could have been found in any other three of the greatest families put together." To this hoard Charles made his own additions.

Apart from the library which will be discussed later, little remains to us of the treasure of the Valois dukes. Most of what is left is now to be seen in the museums and churches of Switzerland, in particular in Bern. This is due to the fact that during their displacements, the dukes encumbered themselves with masses of personal possessions. When Charles set off from Nancy early in 1476 on what was to prove a calamitous military expedition against the Swiss Confederacy, he took along with him the treasury of the Burgundian state and an immense amount of related paraphernalia. Most of this fell into the hands of the Swiss at the rout of Grandson on the shores of the lake of Neuchâtel in March of that year, while what the Burgundians managed to salvage joined the rest of the booty in the disaster of Morat in June. A popular Swiss jingle summed up Charles's losses as follows: "Bij Grandson das Gut, Bij Murten den Mut, Bij Nancy das Blut" ("At Grandson his treasure, at Morat his spirit, at Nancy his blood"). Some of the jewelry from the treasure of the dukes had a picturesque subsequent history, ending up in the most unexpected places. For example, a diamond of 106 carats known as "Le Sancy" found its way to France where it was sold and became part of the crown jewels. It disappeared in 1792 during the looting of the royal possessions, passed into private hands, was sold in London in 1865, and was finally acquired in 1875 by the maharaja of Patiala. It is believed to be still in India today.

An even stranger fate awaited a diamond larger than "Le Sancy" and also taken from Charles at Grandson, known successively as "The Florentine" and "The Tuscan." According to one version it was picked up on the battlefield by a boy who, not knowing what it was, sold it for a few guilders. It was mounted in gold and set with pearls. Whereas in many cases the Swiss, unused to articles of wealth, had little or no idea of the worth of the jewelry and plate which fell into their hands, they realized that this stone must be of considerable value and so could not be appropriated by any single confederate. They accordingly decided to sell it in order to share the proceeds. The first buyer was a Genoese tradesman, from whom it passed in turn to Ludovico Moro and Pope Julius II before coming into the Medici family in the person of Pope Leo X, from whom it acquired the name of "The Florentine." From the next owners, the grand dukes of Tuscany, came its second name, and through them it passed to Duke François of Lorraine who married Maria-Theresa of Austria in 1736. It remained in the imperial treasury in Vienna until 1918, when the last of the Habsburg emperors, Charles, sent it off with other jewels to Switzerland, where it had started its odyssey 450 years earlier. According to one report it was sold by the Austrian government, and while its present whereabouts is unknown, it is believed now to be in an American private collection.

Charles the Bold has been criticized and even ridiculed for

having exposed the Burgundian state treasure to the risks of a military campaign. There is indeed to our eyes something inexplicable and even absurd about such a procedure which multiplied the risks of loss, increased the amount of equipment, horses, and noncombatant personnel required, and correspondingly decreased the mobility of the army. No entirely convincing explanation for this odd habit has been advanced. It had long been a Burgundian custom, it seems, for the duke to be accompanied by his treasure as he moved with his court from residence to residence. The wealth of the duke being also a political instrument, it may have been considered desirable that the duke at all times be in a position to dazzle the enemy or the princes with whom he might enter into negotiations. We have seen that when Charles the Bold went to Trier in 1473, he decked himself out with jewels. In this case it proved a psychological mistake, for while the Burgundians despised the modesty of the emperor's following, both numerically and sartorially, the Germans "despised the pomp and verbiage of said duke, which they attributed to pride." At least a partial explanation for Charles's seeming aberration is that by the time he went off to Switzerland he had been campaigning almost continuously for nearly two years without returning to his palace in Brussels. However, even this does not explain why he set out in the first place to besiege a town on the Rhine with his most precious possessions in his train. Most of the textiles have perished or been dispersed. Fortunately a few fine pieces remain, as well as half a dozen splendid tapestry panels which Bern eventually acquired and which will be discussed later on in this chapter.

Three main factors combine to determine the role to be played by the arts in relation to the fortunes of the Valois dukes. First, Philip the Bold's marriage to the heiress of Flanders opened up to him vast additional sources of wealth when he himself became count of Flanders at the death of his father-in-law in 1384. Second, his idea of building a memorial and a burial place for himself and his descendants in the form of a monastery resulted in an intensive concentration of artistic talent at his capital, Dijon. Third, circumstances prompted him to turn to his northern provinces to find the artists and craftsmen who were to contribute to the decoration of his foundation. The Low Countries had already long been an area of artistic creation. Their influence on the French royal capital had found expression in the development of a Franco-Flemish style in painting, sculpture, manuscript illumination, and tapestry weaving. It was thus natural that Philip should look in that direction for the talent he needed. It was also politic that he should do so, though we do not know whether he was conscious of this factor. At all events, the influx into the duchy of artists from the duke's *pays de par delà* to work on the monument being erected to the glory of the new Burgundian dynasty tended both to symbolize the unity of the administration of the ducal possessions and to imply that an active and successful future lay ahead.

The fame of the charterhouse of Champmol spread far and wide, and visitors from every part of Europe came to see it. The Pope encouraged visits to this praiseworthy act of piety by the duke and granted dispensations to individuals who went on this pilgrimage, thereby fostering the publicity which exalted the magnificence and the power of the ducal house—in stark contrast, it might be added, to the ideals of poverty, austerity, and humility which had inspired Saint Bruno to found his order. By the year 1399, Claus Sluter and his nephew Claus de Werwe had finished the great Calvary in the cloister of Champmol. Thus, even before the fourteenth century had drawn to a close, the reputation of the first Valois duke as a patron of the arts had been established in Christendom and even in Islam. Moreover the Burgundian had also shown himself to be a more active and powerful prince in the realm of politics and war than his brothers of Berry and Anjou. The first in particular tended to subordinate affairs of state to his interest in the pursuit and enjoyment of luxury and beauty. Co-regent of the kingdom of France after 1392, when his nephew Charles VI went out of his mind, Philip the Bold was the most impressive figure of the age in France, and meantime the fortunes of Burgundy prospered. The rule of his son and successor, John the Fearless, lasted fifteen years and was dominated by the political and military consequences of the assassination of his cousin of Orléans in 1407, which he engineered. This gave rise to a bloody struggle for power in the affairs of France between the houses of Burgundy and Orléans and resulted in the assassination of Duke John in 1419 by noblemen in the entourage of the dauphin and in his presence. While work on the decoration of Champmol continued during this period, circumstances were obviously not conducive to a flowering of the arts. The effects of political anarchy in Paris, combined with catastrophic economic deterioration and impoverishment, brought about a sharp decline in orders and in the productivity of craftsmen in all media. It was under the long period of nearly fifty years during which Philip the Good was duke that the splendor and the renown of the Valois dynasty reached its zenith, in both statesmanship and the arts. After Philip's death in 1467, the last ten years of the dynasty under the restless and ambitious Charles the Bold were marked by political and military activities which eclipsed his constructive domestic politics of administrative consolidation, and his interest in the arts, especially music.

At this point, let us take a look at the phenomenon popularly known as "Burgundian art" or "the Burgundian school."

The first question is: Does it exist? If the answer is in the affirmative, the second question must be: What are its identifying characteristics? The term "Burgundian art" is imprecise. It can be taken as referring to the artistic production in all media in the territories ruled, or at various times controlled, by the dukes of Burgundy between 1363 and 1477, from Friesland to the Mâconnais. Or it can be taken as implying that there came into being during that period a distinctive style which originated at the court of the Valois dukes—or under its influence—a style which was Burgundian and not something else, in its origins or at least in its fulfillment, in the same way that, for example, the style of the sculpture of Cluny in the last years of the eleventh century, and of Saulieu, Vézelay, and Autun in the first half of the twelfth century was a style of Romanesque sculpture peculiar to Burgundy and immediately recognizable as such, whether we look at the monuments named above, or at others built in the same general period by monks of the same order in other parts of France or in other countries of Europe. By the time that the Valois dynasty expired, was there, in fact, an artistic style peculiar to the territories which together made up the Burgundian state and which was reflected in all the media?

Between the years 1887 and 1896, a brilliant and forceful French professor named Louis Courajod gave a series of lectures at the École du Louvre in Paris on the history of western art from the dawn of our era to the nineteenth century. It was primarily due to his original and provocative arguments that there emerged the notion of a Burgundian school in the period which interests us. The arguments he advances in order to justify his conclusions are contained in his eighth lecture of the academic year 1888–89, dated February 13, 1889, and entitled, "The Spirit of Burgundian Art." He starts by postulating the existence of an art which he calls "an individual branch of Flemish or Franco-Flemish art," and which "up to a point was for nearly a century, concurrently with Flemish art, the sole art of France." This art, he says, was the successor to the International Gothic style of the close of the fourteenth century, and was distinguished from it by a different spirit. He characterizes this new art as "naïf, tender, both timid and bold." It is not theatrical, nor philosophical, nor literary, nor is it a "courtesan art, nor a slave to the social elements around it." We are told that it is "an intimate art, finding only in a personal and deeply felt inspiration, in a practice devoid of systematic theories and doctrinal convention a singular power, a singular grandeur. It is the art which Flanders and Holland in particular have always practiced. It is the art of the great landscape painters, from the Limburgs and the van Eycks to Ruysdael, Hobbema and the friends of truth, our contemporaries."

All this takes us fairly far afield. It has been quoted at length to show that what Courajod is talking about is not style but inspiration, as the title of the lecture suggests. The founder of this Burgundian school, he goes on to say, was Claus Sluter, and his art, "which filled the fifteenth century, covered France with its products and has continued to exert its influence up to our time." From all that has so far been said on the subject, the only specific characteristic we can attribute to the so-called Burgundian school is that it was inclined to draw its inspiration from nature rather than from traditional stylistic form. In this respect, it was an extension of the art of the Low Countries.

Hitherto, then, we have been given an answer to the first question and have been told that there is such a thing as Burgundian art, but we have been given no characteristics of style by which to identify it. Its only hallmark would appear to be that it is naturalistic rather than formal. But are we then to call all naturalistic art of the fifteenth century Burgundian? Obviously not. In fact, Courajod fails to express in terms of style the aesthetic concept to which he has given the name of a Burgundian school: "In certain places, in certain countries," he goes on to say, "Burgundian art, even in France, once again became purely and simply Flemish," and he completes the circle with the puzzling observation: "For me, the Burgundian period was the most French period of the art of the fifteenth century."

Where does all this leave us? In order to disentangle ourselves from theories and subjective generalities it is best to stick to facts and to go back to the beginning. It was, as Courajod pointed out, the Dutch sculptor Claus Sluter, who introduced to the capital of the duchy of Burgundy a new and highly individual style in the plastic rendering of the human figure in drapery and movement which marked a departure from the stylistic conventions of the late Gothic period, even in its more naturalistic Franco-Flemish phase of the fourteenth century. However, Sluter's contribution to the evolution of plastic art was not only—one may say not principally—a formal one. He invested his subjects with individuality and a power of expression, with an intensity which sets him apart from any other sculptor or artist of his age. "Sluter, we may say," writes Erwin Panofsky, "contains potentially both Michelangelo and Bernini." Now the style of Sluter and his followers owed nothing to Burgundy in terms of its origins. It is only the historical association of the Low Countries with the Burgundian dynasty which has given rise to the practice of terming Burgundian the style which Sluter introduced to Dijon. On the other hand, there is no question whatever about the degree of influence of Sluter and his school on the development of the sculptural style of the fifteenth century—not only in Burgundy and the kingdom of France, but all over Europe. His signature lies in the distinctive harmony of the drapery and in its relationship to the movements of the body, in the role of volume and in the flow of folds which give a complementary emphasis to the mood of the subject. It is the echo of this Sluterian accent in the sculpture of the fifteenth century that has been given the name of a Burgundian school.

While Sluter's style owed nothing to Burgundy, it can also be said that, outside the field of sculpture, Burgundy owed nothing to Sluter either. However, what Sluter did owe to Burgundy, in the person of the duke, was the opportunity to come to Dijon to work on a project which placed him in the limelight. If he had not been given this chance of developing and applying his gifts on a scale and in circumstances which offered him maximum scope and publicity, it is at least debatable whether he would have emerged as a major figure in late medieval art. He set in motion a humanization of the Gothic stylistic conventions which was only fully realized in northern Europe a century later at the time of the Renaissance.

It was also to the Low Countries that Philip the Good turned for painters to work at the decoration of Champmol. Jean Malouel came from Zutphen, Henri Bellechose from Brabant, and Melchior Broederlam from Ypres. It was during his rule that the technique of oil painting was perfected and that easel painting became increasingly popular, both being nurtured by the genius of the brothers van Eyck. One need only recall a few of the names of their followers: Rogier van der Weyden, Dirk Bouts, Hugo van der Goes, Hans Memling, to demonstrate the vitality and the originality of painting in the territories ruled by the Burgundian dukes. Surprisingly enough, the role of Flemish painting (leaving aside manuscript illumination) in the decorative and aesthetic life of the court was smaller than that of sculpture, tapestries, manuscript illumination, and goldsmiths' work.

Orders were placed mostly by wealthy patrons, such as Nicolas Rolin, chancellor of Burgundy, who ordered the polyptich, "The Last Judgment," from Rogier van der Weyden for the chapel of the hospital he founded in Beaune. It was also Nicolas Rolin, not one of the dukes, who had the distinction of being painted both by Jan van Eyck and Rogier van der Weyden. The dukes, although they had painters as members of their household—Jan van Eyck, for example— do not appear to have been as much drawn to this branch of the arts, again excepting manuscript illumination, as they were to others. The principal task of painters at the ducal court seems to have been the decoration of banners, shields, lances, sails of ships, and stage-sets for ceremonies such as banquets and tournaments. In general, Flemish painting owed more to the patronage of the church, noblemen, wealthy officials, merchants, and bankers than it did to the dukes. There is no satisfactory explanation for their apparent lack of interest. The theory has been advanced that painted panels were in the long run less well suited to the continuous displacements of the court and travels of the dukes than were tapestries and manuscripts, but it hardly sounds convincing. One reason might be that portrait painting was still something of an innovation and therefore exceptional. Religious themes continued to be in far greater demand than secular subjects, although demand for the latter increased steadily as the century progressed. The chief outlet for artists long continued to be the decoration of churches, chapels, and religious institutions rather than palaces and private dwellings.

Just as the king's treasure was far richer than those of the dukes of the royal blood, so his library was far larger and more varied. The royal library contained something over one thousand books, the library of the duke of Berry perhaps three hundred, and that of Philip the Bold two hundred or less. While the library of the duke of Berry boasted illuminated manuscripts of supreme quality, Philip's library was particularly strong in French medieval courtly and chivalrous literature and in books on hunting. The only books in Latin—which he did not know—were of a religious nature. He also had several books on the Crusades and on travels to the East. He purchased a number of splendid manuscripts and earned from the authoress Christine de Pisan the appellation of "prince of excelling knowledge." It is likely, however, that this compliment was influenced by the fact that he patronized her work. Philip seems to have kept most of his books in Paris. Others were at Arras, the normal residence of the duchess Margaret. Some, of a religious character, were kept in the ducal chapel at Dijon.

Our information about the ducal libraries is largely derived from the surviving accounts and from the series of inventories which were drawn up between 1404, when Philip the Bold died (followed by an inventory the following year on the death of his wife in Arras), and the period of the reign of Maximilian.

In spite of his short and agitated rule, John the Fearless added to the library he had inherited from his father, so that it numbered 250 or more books at his death. The inventory of 1420 shows that he added to the number of epic tales and chronicles. He also broadened the scope of the subject matter to include translations and adaptations of classical texts, didactic and moralizing works, and some poetry. It is assumed that most of his acquisitions came as heritage from members of his family and by gift. Although he could speak and read Flemish, only five works in that language are listed, most being in French and a few in Latin.

By the time of Philip the Good's death in 1467, his library contained some nine hundred items. It was considered comparable in importance with the other leading libraries of the time, such as those of Pope Nicholas V, of Cosimo de' Medici in Florence, and of Cardinal Bessarion in Venice. It included works in the following fields: biblical, liturgical, philosophical, judicial, didactic, literary, historical, and classical. It also had books about the Turks, travel, and the Golden Fleece. As in so many other respects, the long reign of Philip the Good with its last thirty years of relative peace after the Treaty of Arras was also a golden age for the transcribing and illumination of manuscripts. The library was considered part of the ducal treasure, the manuscripts being under the custody of the keeper of the jewels. The attachment of the dukes to their books was by no means solely determined by their interest in the reading matter. They treasured illuminated manuscripts as works of art combining those same qualities of rarity, beauty, and value which they prized in masterpieces of the other media. One of Philip the Good's favorite authors and copyists, David Aubert, pays tribute to his love for books in the prologue of a chronicle dedicated to him in terms which, though obviously smacking of flattery, at least suggest that Philip welcomed praise for his interest in this branch of the arts and learning generally: "The very renowned and very virtuous prince Philip of Burgundy has long observed the custom of having ancient history read out to him daily; and in order to have at his disposal a library unequaled by any other, he has since his youth employed a number of translators, learned men, expert orators, historians and writers, hard at work in great numbers in various lands; to the point that he is today without any reservation the prince of Christendom who is the best provided with an authentic and rich library, as can be fully ascertained; and while, in the light of his tremendous magnificence, this may be but a small thing, it should nevertheless be a matter of perpetual record, so that all should be aware of his great virtues."

In the early part of Philip's rule, his collection of books increased, thanks largely to bequests, gifts, and purchases. It was not until the middle years of the century that he started placing orders for the transcription of texts and the illumination of books on the scale implied by the above eulogy. The period of greatest activity covers roughly the twenty years between 1445 and 1465, and resulted in a nearly four-fold increase in the size of the library. The moment when the duke took delivery of one of the masterpieces he had ordered was the occasion of a solemn ceremony in the presence of the highest dignitaries. A number of these scenes are depicted in surviving manuscripts. There is no finer example than the frontispiece of the first volume of a manuscript in the Royal Library in Brussels (Ms 9242), representing Philip accepting delivery of a richly bound volume of the *Chronicles of Hainaut*, by Jacques de Guise, from a kneeling figure possibly depicting the translator (from Latin into French) and scribe Jean Wauquelin.

Dressed in black, as usual, and wearing the collar of the Order of the Golden Fleece, the duke stands under the projecting canopy of a richly upholstered throne in a rigid and somewhat mannered pose, suggestive both of the solemnity of the occasion and of his personal authority. The latter is symbolized by a hammer with a long shaft and a small head held in his right hand. He wears a knee-length coat, trimmed with fur and sharply drawn in at the waist, from which his spindly legs project. His feet are encased in shoes with extravagantly long, tapering points. The impression conveyed is one of angularity—both physical and temperamental —in keeping with the stern and supercilious expression of the face surmounted by a massive headdress held in place by a chin strap. At his feet on the tiled floor lies his white whippet. Before him kneels Jean Wauquelin, looking up to him as he holds out the massive volume. On the duke's left, his young son Charles, count of Charolais, stands with head cocked on one side in an acutely observed pose of awkward informality, in delightful contrast to that of his father. Behind him stand several knights of the Golden Fleece. To the duke's right stand the all-powerful chancellor of Burgundy, Nicolas Rolin, and an ecclesiastic thought to be Jean Chevrot, bishop of Tournai. Apart from its exquisite qualities of style and color, this miniature has the merit of evoking with incomparable directness and intensity the personality of Philip the Good and the ceremonial atmosphere of his court.

When Philip placed an order for a book, he took a personal interest in its execution. For example, he asked that the draft text of the *Chronicles of Hainaut* be twice submitted to him, once at Bruges and again at Lille, before giving the translator final authorization to commit it to paper or parchment.

The frontispiece miniature of the second volume depicts the duke and his son listening to the text being read aloud in the company of several courtiers. The frontispiece of the third volume shows Philip paying a visit to David Aubert, who is working at his desk. In addition to Jean Wauquelin, Jean Miélot, and David Aubert (with all of whom the duke placed the greatest number of orders, and whose role— particularly in the case of the last—was equivalent to that of a modern publishing house), many other authors, scribes, and scholars contributed to the production of books for the ducal library.

Philip's interest naturally encouraged a similar taste among members of his court and noble families. Several of them followed his lead and built up their own libraries. Pre-eminent among them was the library of the Great Bastard, Anthony of Burgundy, who is said to have been very much drawn toward *belles histoires*. Some forty volumes from his collection have survived and are today scattered among public and private collections. For example, the city of Breslau owns a splendidly illuminated copy of Froissart's *Chronicle* in four in-folio volumes, with 223 miniatures, in the original black velvet binding. Among other Burgundian noblemen with famous libraries were Jean de Wavrin, Jean de Créquy, the Croy family, and the duke of Cleves. The richest of all excepting that of the dukes belonged to Louis of Bruges. The third wife of Philip the Good, Isabel of Portugal, was also much interested in books. It is possible that an illuminated manuscript now in Brussels (Ms 10308) of the "Mortification of Vain Enjoyments," by René of Anjou, was ordered by her as a present for her husband. Ladies were sensitive to the social advantage of owning a Book of Hours which they considered to be of a quality appropriate to their station in life, and whose display in public during divine service was calculated to arouse the envy and command the respect of others. According to the fifteenth-century poet Eustache Deschamps, one of the ways in which ladies could ruin their husbands was to insist on having such a prayer book:

> *I must have Hours of my Lady*
> *Which are of delicate workmanship,*
> *Of gold and blue, rich and beautiful*
> *Well put together and well painted*
> *Very well bound in fine gold cloth ...*

Philip the Good had a particular fondness for history,

which Froissart had helped to make more accessible by giving it a literary form. The chronicles and translations of ancient texts with which he liked to enrich his library posed new problems of choice of subject matter and pictorial composition for the artists who had to illustrate them. For the illumination of religious texts, the iconographic tradition was well established, and relatively little effort of the imagination was required. The artist merely adopted the choice of scenes which it was customary to illustrate in the type of book on which he was working (Bible, Book of Hours, Psalter, Breviary, etc.) and then modified the composition, if he wished, according to his personal taste and talent. However, when it was a matter of texts for which there was no precedent, entirely new selections of subject matter had to be made, and new compositions had to be invented. This meant that the text had to be read thoroughly and absorbed so that the most significant scenes should be selected and convincingly rendered.

In the absence of illustrations it is unprofitable to discuss questions of style. We need only note that several influences, some indigenous, some derived from France and Italy, are reflected in the illuminations of manuscripts in the northern possessions of the dukes of Burgundy. In spite of this, a certain unity is achieved, reflecting rather a courtly mood and vision of the world than a style characteristic of Burgundian court production. The painstaking emphasis on detail in every object that meets the eye does more than inform us about the appearance of things and people of the time. We are given an insight into the contemporary way of living of the rich and the poor, the mighty and the modest, into the atmosphere of life at the ducal court, into the moods, manners, and tastes of the fifteenth century. The effect of court patronage on scribes and illuminators was to stimulate competition among them and thus to release the full potential of their talent. The major centers of book production for the ducal library all lay in the northern possessions: Hesdin, Amiens, Valenciennes, Brussels, Audenarde, and Bruges, the last becoming the most important of them all in the last ten years of the life of Philip the Good.

After his father's death Charles the Bold ordered the completion of several manuscripts which were still unfinished. Like Philip, he was interested in history, but the nature of the difference between the two interests reflected the difference between the two temperaments. Whereas his father sought in history lessons of wisdom and the teachings of experience, Charles was attracted by the heroic side of life. He had been an eager student with a romantic interest in tales of the Knights of the Round Table and other legends of the dawn of chivalry, but as he grew older he turned increasingly to heady accounts celebrating personal glory and military triumphs in Greek and Roman history. He had a predilection for Alexander the Great, son of another Philip. A contemporary notes that "he derived pleasure only from the history of Rome and the deeds of Julius Caesar, Pompey and Hannibal, Alexander the Great, and other such great and famous men whom he wished to follow and to emulate." When he raised his eyes from his books, he could see the exploits of his heroes recorded on a large scale and in bright colors on the tapestries which covered the walls. In order to satisfy his tastes, he brought together a team of translators and writers to produce copies of his favorite authors. He too liked to be read to in the evening, and doubtless his dreams were often peopled with the heroic deeds of the past which he projected into his own future.

About 350 manuscripts from the library of Philip the Good have survived. Nearly 250 of them are in the Royal Library in Brussels, established in 1559 by King Philip II to house the ducal books. Nearly 200 of the finest items were appropriated by Louis XV after the French had taken Brussels in 1746. Further depredations occurred during the wars of the French Revolution. After the Congress of Vienna, a number of the manuscripts were returned to Brussels by France, but several dozen of them remain in various libraries in Paris to this day. Considering the hazards to which they have been exposed, it is almost miraculous that not more than 550 manuscripts should have been lost in the course of five centuries.

"Born under the eyes of princes who normally expect only compliments," writes a historian, "the literature of Burgundy habitually bows and scrapes before them in the most deferent of attitudes." Implicit in this too sweeping criticism is the truthful observation that Burgundian literature consists largely of chronicles of the times subsidized by the dukes. In other words, the originality and the vitality of the art of manuscript illumination and the industry of the scribes, copyists, translators, and adaptors of texts were not matched by the growth of a Burgundian literary school. The style of the chroniclers has been the target of later critics, particularly French. One suspects a touch of nationalistic irritation in their reaction to the massive records of the achievements of the dukes, thanks to which, as one French historian put it, "history became Burgundian." The style of the court historians has been termed cumbrous, heavy, involved, and diffuse—and so it is, compared with the refinement and elegance of a later age. But what makes these chroniclers precious to us is directness of observation and vividness of detail in accounts of events and of life around them. Their defects of style are those of their age.

The increasing tendency of Burgundian authors to transcribe romances from verse into prose as the fifteenth century advanced was in response to changes in the reading tastes of the age, for "today, great princes and other lords prefer prose to rhyme," a contemporary tells us, "because the language is fuller and is not as constricted."

There is little to say on the subject of poetry in the times of the Valois dukes. Charles d'Orléans and François Villon belong to France: they owed nothing to the Burgundian court. Literary production consisted largely, as we have noted, of translations from ancient authors, and the purpose was to educate rather than to please or charm. Being increasingly imbued with the history and the legends of antiquity, the intellectual atmosphere of the court served to prepare the ground for the time when the seed of humanism of the Renaissance would be planted in France toward the close of the century. A current of literary taste running parallel to that flowing from antiquity drew its inspiration from the romantic aspects of chivalry, expressed in such compilations as the "Geste des ducs de Bourgogne" and in accounts of the deeds of valor accomplished by Jacques de Lalaing, the embodiment of the knightly ideal of the ages. This mood expressed itself at court in the form of banquets and tournaments, of which examples are given in Chapter VI.

A more earthy and natural Burgundian taste finds expression in a collection of one hundred more or less bawdy stories called *The Hundred New Tales.* We know the names of thirty-six of the contributors, the most prominent of whom is referred to as "Monseigneur" (Philip the Good himself), by whose order the tales were assembled and published. Among the forms of entertainment which Philip enjoyed was the telling of tales of romantic adventure by members of his circle of intimate companions. Even in an age when strict religious devotion often went hand in hand with extreme licentiousness, Philip was notorious for the degree to which he suffered from what a contemporary termed "the vice of the flesh." He had some thirty recorded mistresses and an unrecorded number of bastard offspring. This lusty propensity is given free rein in these tales, whose literary genre originated with Boccaccio. Although some of them are merely coarse and dull, others are amusing. Their language is direct and colloquial in contrast to the pompous style of court literature. They give the reader an insight into the mentality of the people of the time at varying levels of society. They convey a sense of what life was like, how human beings reacted to situations and behaved toward each other, and what their sense of humor was.

All in all the role of literature under the Valois dukes of Burgundy was a modest one. Their merit lay in having stimulated an interest in books and in having built up a splendid library with an ever-widening range of subject matter, thus contributing to the intellectual, as well as the artistic, development of the late Middle Ages.

When we try to visualize the surroundings in which noblemen and wealthy officials of the court lived in the late fourteenth and fifteenth centuries, we must imagine the walls of the great rooms in their castles hung with large tapestries. Hangings with religious subjects were also woven for churches. Magnificent as decoration, tapestries reflected the taste and preference in subject matter of the most wealthy and powerful elements in the land. In turn they influenced the ideas and values of those who lived among them and saw them day after day.

The two media of tapestry and fresco painting had, broadly speaking, the same function, and evolved to a certain extent in parallel fashion and timing. They were both vulnerable, though in different ways: while the survival of wall paintings depended chiefly on the fate of the building of which they were a part and the climatic conditions to which they were exposed, tapestries were subject to wear and tear and the ravages of moths and damp. While tapestries had the advantage of mobility—thus being seen by a greater number of people—the chances of their being damaged or destroyed were correspondingly increased. Unfortunately only a very small proportion of the production of the looms of the Middle Ages has been preserved. What remains provides us with a lively, brilliant, and detailed view—usually on a large scale— of courtly life in northern Europe at the time of our dukes. Whatever might be the period in which the events represented were supposed to be taking place, the fashions, the architecture, and the objects depicted were those of the times in which the tapestries were woven. The exploits of Hercules, the legend of the Golden Fleece, the story of Alexander, and the triumphs of Caesar—all were cast in contemporary fashion. When Philip the Good married Isabel of Portugal at Bruges in 1430, he dispatched fifteen cartloads of tapestries there for this event. Similar displacements occurred on frequent occasions, thus expanding greatly the range of influence of new stylistic developments in a region, or in a center of production of tapestry. It is probable that this increased mobility, which accompanied the growing production of and demand for tapestries from the middle of the fourteenth century onward, contributed to the formation toward the end of the century of a certain unity in the art of Europe, which we call the International Gothic style.

Here again, as in the case of all other artistic media, tapestry weaving was enormously stimulated by the orders placed by the Burgundian dukes and the members of their court. When Philip the Bold became duke in 1363, both Paris and Arras were flourishing centers of weaving, the latter in particular being renowned for the quality of its yarn, spun from the finest English wool. In the early years of the fifteenth century, the records of Arras carry the names of some seventy weavers. The name of the town itself became synonymous with the word tapestry. The marketing of the product of the looms was usually in the hands of middlemen who solicited and placed orders, and generally conducted an export-import business in all kinds of cloths and costly fabrics. The tapestry dealers of Paris and Arras co-operated closely: wholesalers from each town entered into partnership and were sometimes citizens simultaneously both of Paris and of Arras.

Tapestries, requiring the contribution of designers, highly skilled labor, and the finest quality of woolen thread (sometimes combined, in the more sumptuous ones, with silk, gold, and silver threads), cost a great deal to make and could only be afforded by the wealthiest individuals and institutions. They were highly prized and considered as gifts fit for kings and emperors. After the catastrophe of the Franco-Burgundian crusade at Nicopolis in 1396, the Turkish sultan Bayazid let it be known to Philip the Bold that Arras tapestries would be acceptable as part of the huge ransom required to free the duke's son, provided they represented interesting subjects from ancient legends. Among those sent to the sultan was a series illustrating the story of Alexander the Great. A set on the same subject ordered in 1459 at Tournai by Philip the Good cost him five thousand gold ducats.

Philip the Bold ordered tapestries both in Paris and in Arras with a wide range of subject matter: biblical, classical, mythological, and legendary; also contemporary chivalrous romances, allegorical and moralistic tales, as well as idyllic and pastoral subjects. He had a particular fondness for scenes of hawking and the chase.

Given the small number of tapestries from that period

which have survived, it seems worthwhile to draw the reader's attention to one or two examples that can be seen today which give an idea of the scale and the beauty of these great hangings in design and color. In the Victoria and Albert Museum in London are four huge tapestries dating from the second third of the fifteenth century, with hunting scenes, formerly the property of the dukes of Devonshire. They have been cleaned and carefully restored and are splendid examples of the kind of decoration we are discussing. These tapestries may possibly have been woven for the marriage of Margaret, daughter of King René of Anjou, and King Henry VI of England.

In the Historical Museum in Bern, Switzerland, are preserved several exceptionally fine examples of Burgundian tapestries. These have been in the town's possession since the first half of the sixteenth century. One panel woven in wool, silk, and gold thread and measuring some eleven by five feet, is of particular importance: it is a woven replica of scenes illustrating the spirit of Justice which Rogier van der Weyden painted between 1432 and 1445 for the west wall of the Golden Chamber, which was also used as the Court of Justice, of the town hall of Brussels. The originals were unhappily destroyed by a fire in 1695. Together with the altarpiece of the Mystic Lamb in Ghent by the brothers van Eyck, these panels were formerly considered to be the most famous paintings in the Low Countries.

In the same museum is a set of four panels woven in wool and silk which tell the story of Julius Caesar from the time he left Gaul after his victories there to his triumphal entry into Rome as absolute ruler. Woven into the panels are verses taken from a compilation entitled *Deeds of the Romans*, originating in the thirteenth century but retranscribed later. Illuminated copies of this work were in the ducal library, and we can assume that they were read by Charles the Bold, who, as has been said, was particularly fond of stories about the heroes of antiquity. Some scholars believe that this set of panels was commissioned personally by him. When he made his formal entry into Arras in 1468, scenes from the *Deeds of the Romans* were acted in mime in the streets of that town, which may have suggested to Charles the idea of ordering a set of tapestries on this subject. The composition of the four panels suggests that they were intended to hang in pairs facing each other, possibly as decoration for a Burgundian throne room.

The dukes of Burgundy were also particularly attached to the story of the Trojan War and the deeds of its heroes, from whom, as French princes of the royal blood, they also claimed descent. The inventory of the ducal library in 1467 at Philip's death lists seventeen manuscripts concerning the Trojan legend, and the duke had ordered a compilation of these from his chaplain, Raoul Lefèvre. It is possible that when Charles the Bold and Margaret of York were married in Bruges the following year, a series of the history of Troy, offered to Charles the Bold by the city and the franc, or castellany (region around the city and controlled by it), of Bruges, and first mentioned in the financial accounts a few years later, hung on the walls of the palace. The special importance of the story of Troy is reflected in the name chosen for the ship on which Margaret sailed from England to the Low Countries: the *New Ellen*. In 1469, Margaret herself commissioned William Caxton to translate the *Recueil* or compilation mentioned above from the manuscripts he had found in the ducal library. The first printed book in the English language proved to be *The Recuyell of the Histories of Troy*, dedicated to the duchess by Caxton and printed by him in Bruges in 1473.

Heroes of contemporary history were also honored, such as Bertrand du Guesclin, constable of France in the late fourteenth century, whom Philip the Bold particularly admired. Burgundian victories were recorded, such as that over the militia of Ghent in 1382 and that of John the Fearless over Liège a quarter of a century later.

Cartoons for tapestries were often based on compositions taken from miniatures in illuminated manuscripts. Up to a certain point there is some similarity between the illustration of books and tapestry decoration. However, the medium of weaving on a large scale evolved in accordance with its own technical and aesthetic exigencies. Moreover, tapestries were the product of teamwork, not of an individual artist, and this fact accounts for a certain conservatism in style. Orders placed by the dukes had a particularly strong influence on the taste of the times over a period of many years. Sometimes several sets of tapestries were woven from a single cartoon, thus increasing the distribution of the formula which reflected the taste of the court.

All four dukes displayed a strong personal interest in tapestries. Philip the Bold used to inspect the cartoons personally, and he sometimes nominated the artist he wanted to carry out the work. He had an expert in weaving as a *valet de chambre* in his household, while a team of weavers known as "guardians of the tapestries" was responsible for their safety, upkeep, and repair. In the fifty years following Philip the Bold's death, the number of tapestries had so greatly increased from the seventy-five he had left behind that the staff needed for their care had to be enlarged and special warehouses built to store them.

By the end of the first third of the fifteenth century, the importance of Paris as a weaving center and as a market for Arras tapestries had much declined for reasons already noted. Even though Philip the Good continued to place some orders in Arras, it was rapidly being overtaken in importance by

Tournai. Among the factors favoring this French enclave in Burgundian territory were direct access by water to Antwerp and the good fortune of having had two bishops in succession (Jean Chevrot, 1436–60, and Guillaume Fillastre, 1460–73), who were both patrons of the arts and who greatly stimulated the activity of local looms, both by their own orders and by those they attracted. It was Jean Chevrot in particular who first established close relations with the ducal court which were to prove highly beneficial to the weaving industry of Tournai. We have already mentioned his possible identification with the figure standing on the right of Chancellor Nicolas Rolin in the miniature in the *Chronicles of Hainaut*. From 1446 onward ducal orders were placed in Tournai. It is possible that the hangings for the beds of the Hôtel-Dieu in Beaune were woven there. The founder of the hospital, Nicolas Rolin, owned a tapestry bearing his arms and representing the popular theme of peasants and woodcutters at their labors in a wood, of which several sets were disposed of by the chief tapestry merchant of Tournai, Pasquier Grenier. An example of this particular kind of tapestry is now in the Museum of Decorative Arts in Paris.

The passion of Philip the Good, and even more of his successor, for identifying themselves with the qualities and the prestige of heroes of the ancient world found a prodigiously effective outlet in great woven compositions. In propaganda terms, these played a role corresponding to that of modern advertising by constantly and dramatically reminding people that legend and history lived again in the person and the attributes of the duke. The hints sometimes left nothing to the imagination: in two panels now in the Palazzo Doria in Rome, which probably once formed part of the set of the story of Alexander already mentioned, Alexander's parents are represented with the features of Philip the Good and Isabel of Portugal, while the Count of Charolais can easily be recognized in the features given to Alexander himself. In a no doubt intentionally untactful reminder to his "*beau cousin*," Louis XI, of the position which the House of Burgundy had arrogated to itself in the general scheme of things, Philip the Good had this, or another similar set hung in his Paris residence on the occasion of the newly crowned king's formal entry into his capital in 1461. When Charles the Bold set out to dazzle the emperor Frederick III in Trier in 1473, he took this set with him. However, if the latter saw it, it failed to produce the hoped-for effect on him.

As in the case of all the other arts, music suffered from the disruption and general impoverishment of life in France as the Hundred Years' War dragged on. Burgundy, on the other hand, now included parts of northeastern France and Flanders, which had long been the principal musical center of Europe, although there were also important schools of music in England and in Italy. The dukes of Burgundy were very fond of music, and they had the means, as well as the opportunity, to attract the best musicians and composers to their court. They founded the institution of the ducal chapel, whose fame spread even beyond Europe. Thus music, too, contributed to the prestige enjoyed by Burgundy and to the furtherance of the political aims of its rulers.

In the first thirty years of the fifteenth century, music, in conformity with the trend in the visual arts, acquired an increasingly European character. It was at the Burgundian court that musical style and fashion underwent a significant change. Under the influence of composers from the northern territories such as Guillaume Dufay and Gilles Binchois, the traditional music of chivalry gradually died away to be replaced by the new polyphonic style of composition, in which a number of parts, each forming an individual melody, combine simultaneously and harmonize with each other. Indeed, the first sixty years of the fifteenth century have been called "the age of Dufay" by music historians. Various political developments fostered currents of exchanges between north and south: the exile of the popes in Avignon opened and broadened channels between the French-speaking lands and Italy, just as the music of England, whose leading light was John Dunstable, came to the Continent in the wake of the victories of Henry V. In the last quarter of the century the marriage between the heiress to Burgundy and the heir to the imperial crown was responsible for the extension of the music of the Burgundian court to Austria, where Maximilian founded a chapel at Innsbruck with musicians from his northern possessions.

The virtuosity on instruments and the singing of the people of the Low Countries particularly impressed their contemporaries. It would almost seem that those who may call themselves Burgundians have a natural propensity toward the enjoyment of drink and the consequent vocal expression of their pleasure. Whereas the original Burgundians, as we have mentioned above, were notorious for the raucousness of their voices, those who bore their name a thousand years later had greatly refined their art. A contemporary Italian praises the Flemish choristers who, "having drunk good wine, begin to sing with vibrant voices, the which their throats may very easily send forth as they are all strong and robust in the chest." Of one singer, the same source writes, "You would say on hearing him that he must be a Fleming, for his gullet is disposed as [if] it were a great organ pipe," thanks to which he is able to sing "down to the bottom of the cellar."

The fame of Dufay spread early, and this brought him the opportunity to travel widely. He was already popular at the court of Rimini when barely twenty years old and was commissioned to compose the music for the wedding of a son of the Byzantine emperor Manuel Palaeologus to Cleophe Malatesta. In 1436 he composed a motet for the consecration of the cathedral of Florence. Though a priest and canon both of Cambrai and Mons, he was for some time a member of the papal chapel, and he also visited England. The range of his compositions was wide, for in addition to sacred music he composed secular songs, ballads, roundelays, etc., and he put some of Petrarch's verses to music. Throughout his life he continuously enriched the musical mode of expression by developing its responsiveness to human moods and emotions as well as by broadening its technical range. It was largely thanks to Dufay, to his pupil Gilles Binchois, and to the Englishman John Dunstable that music became more expressive of the personality of the composer. Whereas Dunstable restricted himself to religious compositions, Binchois wrote both the text and the music of many of the *chansons* attributed to him. These have been termed "the oldest genuine examples of the union of poetry and music in accompanied song." He also set to music poems by contemporary authors such as Duke Charles of Orléans, Alain Chartier, and Christine de Pisan. The followers of Dufay and Binchois, of whom the most famous are Ockeghem and Josquin des Prés, further developed the polyphonic mode. Though mostly born in the Low Countries and hence Burgundian subjects, they were in fact thoroughly international, many of them spending their lives abroad, Ockeghem himself remaining for more than forty years in the French royal chapel.

Music flourished in the great northern towns of Antwerp, Bruges, and Cambrai, and was supported financially by wealthy citizens. Cathedral choirs played an important role in the evolution of musical style and in the musical training of the young. If one adds to this musical bent the sustained patronage and personal interest of the dukes, it is not surprising that the Low Countries should have become, according to H. J. Moser, "the magnetic pole of composition" in Europe.

Already in the late fourteenth century, Philip the Bold had participated in the creation of a kind of fraternity consisting of those members of both the royal and the ducal courts who were musically and poetically inclined. At its gatherings minstrels and poets could display their talent and benefit from being exposed to that of others. It was called the *Cour d'Amour* or *Cour amoureuse* and it had a "Prince of Love" at its head. Pierre de Hauteville, one of Philip the Bold's squires, was its master from its inception and continued to play an active role in it through the reign of John the Fearless and well into that of Philip the Good. Its principal feast was on Saint Valentine's Day, when a mass was celebrated. These romantic musical assemblies, at which the more tender sounds of strings, flutes, and harps were to be heard instead of trumpets and brasses, continued long to be held at the Burgundian court, one in Brussels as late as 1460.

The quality and the influence of music at the Burgundian court reached their peak under the last two dukes. There was another reason besides the duke's liberality toward musicians which helped to explain the extent to which music flourished under Philip the Good. He was personally extremely exigent and discriminating in the selection of the members of his chapel, to whom he used to give a personal audition. That this was by no means a mere formality is shown by the fact that in the year 1446 he listened to, and turned down, a chaplain of the duke of Savoy, another of the bishop of Liège, and the choirmaster of the boys' choir of Antwerp cathedral as well. In chapter II reference is made to the choir school he founded at Dijon, in addition to his private chapel. He did the same thing at Lille. At both schools a music master and a master of grammar taught descant, counterpoint, and Latin. Music was much in fashion among, and greatly prized by, all men of high estate. Charles of Orléans, who had cultivated his delicate poetic inspiration during the twenty-five years he spent as a prisoner in London after the battle of Agincourt, had a robe made for himself after his return to freedom in 1440, on the sleeves of which were embroidered the text and the score of a song entitled, "Madam, I feel happier," the music set forth in 568 pearls.

We shall see in a later chapter the often curious role played by music in court festivities and banquets. In fact the duke's life was punctuated by an almost incessant musical accompaniment. Nearly his every move called for the appropriate musical emphasis. In wartime as in peacetime, his comings and goings were perpetually announced—whether it was the blare of trumpets, the entertainment of his minstrels, or the gentler harmonies of his chapel. Philip the Good was particularly fond of his trumpeters, whom he prized above his other minstrels. The trumpet was the instrument of heraldry and nobility *par excellence*. The trumpeters announced the presence of the prince and proclaimed his power and his glory to the skies; the louder the sound, the greater the impression made on those present: "And these minstrels sounded so loud that one could not have heard the thunder of God," notes Christine de Pisan approvingly. When the duke paid a formal visit to one of his good towns, he was naturally preceded by his trumpeters, and he was usually greeted by staged allegorical tableaux, often of bizarre fantasy. For example, in 1458 on the occasion of his "joyous entry" into Ghent, on which he had inflicted a bloody defeat but a few years previously, he was met by an elephant with a castle on its back, from which two men and four children sang the following song of propitiatory—if insincere—welcome:

> *"Long live Burgundy" is our cry,*
> *So be it in thought and deed.*
> *None other shall we have, for thus we feel,*
> *And thus we wish it ever to be . . .*
> *All together, we pray you, let us sing*
> *To his great and joyous entry.*
> *"Long live Burgundy" . . .*
> *Let us rejoice for him*
> *Who has come to the lands he owns,*
> *Thanks to whom our sorrows are over,*
> *By crying with a single heart*
> *"Long live Burgundy."*

It seems to have been the accepted practice of the times to remind the population of a town visited by the duke of the honor of his presence among them by sounding instruments through the night. When Philip visited Utrecht in 1456, the night watch was kept by Burgundian noblemen from his entourage, and "trumpets and bugles and loud instruments . . . did not cease sounding all night," this having allegedly been much appreciated by the population.

When the duke traveled abroad, he was saluted by the musicians of the court of the sovereign through whose lands he was passing, as well as by those of the towns on his way. Jealous of their prerogatives, the trumpeters of the emperor prevailed on him to forbid the municipal authorities to employ trumpeters or cymbalists for their official greetings. This practice seems also to have been observed in Burgundy, but in 1433, Dijon petitioned the duke to authorize it to use a trumpet for its public proclamations rather than a horn "because several noblemen and strangers laugh at the horn as not being *'une chose honneste,'* and it would be a greater honor for the town to have a trumpet than a horn." Philip granted this request the following year.

Charles the Bold learned to play the harp as a child, and was in general inclined toward the gentler musical instruments—in contrast to his temperament as an adult. He learned composition and liked to sing, but unfortunately nature had not endowed him with an agreeable voice. On October 23, 1460, a motet of his composition was sung in his presence. He spent a great deal in gifts to musicians, and in 1465 he persuaded his father to let his English chaplain, Robert Morton, spend five months with him. As soon as he became duke, he engaged three lutenists as members of his household, and he invited Robert Morton to be present at his wedding to Margaret of York.

When he laid siege to the town of Neuss in 1474, he relieved the tedium by having his entire chapel and all his minstrels with him at his camp, where, writes a contemporary observer, they "engendered such delectable harmony that they banished all melancholy, created fresh joy and raised all fainting hearts to the throne of perfect bliss. In the duke's quarters, in particular, at the appointed hours, the sound to be heard was so pleasant that it seemed to be an earthly paradise, more divine than human. And as Orpheus broke down the gates of Hell with the sound of his harp, so the modulations of these musical instruments tempered the bitterness of the rude Saxon hearts and lulled the enemy to sleep with its delightful euphony"—not, be it noted, sufficiently to permit Charles to capture the town.

Charles, writes the same chronicler, loved music as much as any other man, and rightly so, he goes on to say, "for music is the resonance of the skies, the voice of angels, the joy of Paradise, the spirit of the air, the instrument of the Church, the song of little birds, recreation for all sad and sorrowing hearts, the persecution and banishment of devils." He also notes that the duke "brought together the most famous musicians in the world and maintained a Chapel graced with such harmonious and delectable voices that next to celestial glory, there was nothing as blissful."

Thus, in the words of contemporaries, did the Grand Dukes of the West appreciate and render homage to the art of music!

CHAPTER V

The Order of the Golden Fleece

O F all the political and psychological initiatives taken by the dukes with the aim of strengthening their position internationally as well as domestically, none was more immediately and permanently successful than the creation by Philip the Good of the Order of the Golden Fleece on the occasion of his marriage to Isabel of Portugal at Bruges on January 10, 1430.

Contrary to some theories, this was no hasty improvisation —far from it: "The institution of the Golden Fleece," writes the contemporary court chronicler Georges Chastellain, "had long been considered in secret by the duke, but was not revealed until this hour." Nor is there any truth in the speculation that the choice of the Golden Fleece was in allusion to the golden locks of a girl from Bruges who had conferred her favors on the duke, though it must be admitted that his well-deserved reputation for gallantry at least lent a measure of plausibility to the rumor.

To achieve the greatest possible publicity for a step to which he rightly attached much importance, Philip chose a time when the eyes of Europe were upon him for his announcement. His aim was to mobilize the conscience of Christendom under his personal leadership and to launch a victorious crusade to free the Holy Places from the Turks.

Ever since the thirteenth century the institution of chivalry had steadily been declining from what has been defined as "the ideal expression of the Christian fervor of the noble-hearted warrior, steeped in faith, living under God, and ever ready to wield his sword in defense of a just cause." This deterioration, both spiritual and military had been reflected in the decadence of the military monastic orders, and it largely explains the final extinction of the crusading spirit. In place of a natural dedication to collective action in the name of an ideal, there had emerged a spirit of individual rivalry, of competition for public acclaim and the favor of ladies. The art of war had become increasingly an instrument at the service of ambitious princes pursuing personal policies, who cultivated it as a sport for their own advancement. Attempts had been made to revive the chivalrous spirit by the creation of various orders and brotherhoods designed to infuse their members with a sense of common purpose and idealism and to link them to each other and to the ruling prince by an oath of loyalty and service. Among these, the most illustrious was the Order of the Garter, founded by Edward III of England in 1348.

From the start, the Valois dukes had shown great interest in the idea of a crusade, but the experience of Philip the Bold had not been a happy one. A crusade against the Turks in 1396 in response to an appeal from the king of Hungary and led nominally by Philip's young son, the future John the Fearless, ended in disaster under the walls of Nicopolis in the Danubian plain. This expedition against an aggressive, experienced, and numerically superior enemy had been light-heartedly undertaken. There had been wild talk among the young noblemen, many of them mere youths, about driving the Turk back into Asia and freeing the Holy Places. In fact, the flower of the knighthood of France and Burgundy perished in battle or was put to the sword, except for a handful, the future duke among them, who were kept as prisoners to be freed only by exorbitant ransoms.

A northern French knight, Philippe de Mézières, who had served the Lusignan family in Cyprus, had been so impressed by the growing power and threat of Islam that he had attempted, though without success, to establish an "Order of Knighthood of the Passion of Jesus Christ," whose goal was the revival of the crusading spirit on an international scale. After Nicopolis, he wrote a "Lamentable and Consolatory Epistle" to Philip the Bold in which he expounded his ideas in terms later echoed in the statutes of the Order of the Golden Fleece. The short and politically stormy rule of John the Fearless was unpropitious for the creation of new institutions, but the ideas of de Mézières found fertile ground in the person of the next duke, whose epitaph on his tomb at Dijon included the lines:

In order to uphold the Church which is the House of God,
I created the noble Order, known as the Fleece.

The Burgundian court continued to pay close attention to the situation in the Near East, and to concern itself with the welfare of the Christian community in Palestine as well as with the protection and upkeep of the Holy Places. Shortly after becoming duke, Philip the Good sent two noblemen to collect information in Syria and Palestine. One of them also went to Constantinople and to Adrianople in order to gather political and military intelligence on the Turks. Burgundian galleys played a role in naval actions in the defense of Rhodes, and Burgundian ships sailed the waters of the Danube and the Black Sea. Thus Philip the Good, when he urged the French king Charles VII to mount and lead a crusade, had long been aware of, and well informed on, the threat to the survival of Christendom posed by Turkish power coupled with the increasing weakness of the Byzantine position. He pledged to support Charles (or anyone else he might delegate in his place), both in person and materially. However, France's domestic problems, in particular her economic situation in the last part of the Hundred Years' War, precluded such a venture which, moreover, would have entailed the absence of the king from his country—a risk not to be run lightly.

As for Philip, he had his own problems to face at home: the task of the consolidation and administration of the expanding Burgundian territories in the face of the resistance of the northern merchant cities to his centralizing policies. An uprising by Ghent was not finally put down by him until 1453, the year of the fall of Constantinople. Nonetheless, on hearing the news, Philip at once thought of mounting a crusade with the liberation of Constantinople as its immediate goal. In view of the formidable scale of such an undertaking and of the relative dearth of resources required to give it even the semblance of a chance of success, the sincerity of the duke's intentions in proclaiming his desire to embark on such a project has been generally questioned. "In the case of Philip the Good," writes one historian, "the design of a crusade seems to have been a mixture of chivalrous caprice and political advertising; he wished to pose, by this pious and useful project, as the protector of Christendom to the detriment of the king of France." There is no question of the alertness of the dukes to any opportunity to promote their interests. This consideration has always been a factor in framing national policy, in our age as much as in the past. However, it seems unnecessarily gratuitous and even implausible to attribute Philip's initiative after the fall of Constantinople solely to narrow motives of self-interest. The threat posed to the West by the fall to Islam of the bastion which had for so long assured its security was real enough. It was not until 230 years later that the Turkish menace was to be finally eliminated under the walls of Vienna. In fact, Burgundy was the only European power in the middle of the fifteenth century with the political will, the energy, and the means to attempt the task of mobilizing the resources required for such an enterprise. The fortunes of England, on the eve of the Wars of the Roses were, like those of France, at a low ebb financially and politically; while the empire—impoverished, divided, and weakly ruled—was in no condition even to attempt to play a role in any international undertaking.

The timing of the announcement of the decision to create the new order also offered Philip the opportunity to assert a greater degree of independence vis-à-vis England. His ally the duke of Bedford, English regent of France in the name of the infant king Henry VI, was also his brother-in-law, and it was he who offered Philip membership in the Order of the Garter. However, Philip was reluctant to accept an honor which would have bound him by oath even more closely to the crown of England. At the same time he wished to avoid offending the English by an unadorned refusal. He accordingly told Bedford that he was unfortunately not in a position to accept his flattering offer because he himself intended to found an order which he had already been discussing with his advisers and it would not be proper for him to go back on his decision. The excuse was accepted and Philip seized the best moment to make his decision public. That the announcement created a profound impression is shown by the fact that the county of Flanders voted a subsidy of 100,000 crowns for the establishment of the new order. According to the proclamation, its purposes were to revere God, to uphold the Christian faith, to honor and exalt the noble order of chivalry, to honor former worthy knights, to encourage present knights to conduct themselves even more worthily, and to incite those who were to become members to acquire a good reputation and never to make themselves liable to exclusion from membership.

The first chapter was held nearly a year and a half later, on November 22, 1431, at Lille, where the statutes comprising sixty-six articles were formally promulgated. Also, on this occasion the number of knights admitted to membership was raised from the original figure of twenty-four (in addition to the duke himself) to thirty-one in all.

The proclamation specified that the "order and confraternity of knighthood and amicable association of a certain number of knights" had been named after the Golden Fleece which Jason had captured, and that it had been established in reverence of the Blessed Virgin Mary and of Saint Andrew, patron saint of Burgundy. It is possible that Philip had been inspired by a tapestry of the story of Jason, which he had inherited from his father, and by *The History of Troy*, a historical treatise beginning with the history of the Argonauts and the capture of the Golden Fleece. These may have turned his thoughts toward the idea of a maritime expedition to the Near East in order to recover the Holy Places and, incidentally, to avenge the humiliation of Nicopolis.

As soon as the creation of the new order had been announced, the duke informed Pope Eugene IV that its knights would always devote themselves with all their might to the defense of the church. The Pope responded most favorably, issuing three bulls approving and confirming the order; and the Council of Bâle which convened shortly thereafter sang its praises.

However, it was not long before the church started becoming restless because of the discrepancy between the order's lofty inspiration and goals, on the one hand, and the unedifying moral conduct of the hero of the Argonauts, who had violated his pledge to Medea. Already at the first chapter,

Jean Germain, bishop of Nevers and first chancellor of the order, had formulated religious and moral objections to the selection of Jason as its sponsor. He proposed instead the name of Gideon, also associated with the story of a fleece, but one which had been the object of a double miracle recorded in the Bible and which had heralded a victory over the Midianites, just as this biblical fleece would, as the emblem of the order, herald a victory over the infidel. Moreover, the purity of the fleece impregnated with the dew of heaven would symbolize the purity of the Blessed Virgin, to whom the order was dedicated. In 1448, an order was placed with the looms of Tournai for a set of eight tapestries illustrating the story of Gideon, which would henceforth decorate the halls in which chapters of the order were held. These were hung for the first time in the present Hall of the Knights at The Hague, in which the ninth chapter of the order was held in 1456, with Charles, still count of Charolais, presiding. However, as we shall see in the next chapter, the memory of Jason had by no means been eclipsed as late as 1454. The hero of Colchis, in fact, continued to find supporters up to the end of the rule of Philip the Good. By that time another chancellor of the order, Guillaume Fillastre, had managed to unearth no fewer than four additional fleeces with which edifying knightly virtues could be associated.

The statutes of the order bound the members to follow closely the lead of the duke as its chief and sovereign. One article specified that if he or any of his successors decided to take up arms in defense of the Christian faith or in behalf of the Holy See, the knights were obligated to serve him in person.

In addition to the advantages which it brought the duke on the international scene, the order contributed effectively to forging unity between the diversified Burgundian territories, few of which had previously had anything in common with each other. By forming an elite corps bound by oath and with a sense of common purpose, a dynastic link was established between the various families. This strengthened the duke's hand in dealing with attempts of the major towns to resist his policies and to retain their privileges and autonomy. The duke pledged himself to consult with the knights before embarking on military ventures or taking any other far-reaching measures. This concession, however, was more formal than substantive and did not mean that the duke's will could be effectively resisted. At all events, the order was something more than a mere association of representatives of the chivalrous tradition dedicated to the maintenance and practice of knightly virtues and ideals. It constituted a political and social oligarchy loyal to the duke and thus, by its function, an instrument of his policies. Under Charles the Bold the knights were granted access to the ducal grand council, thereby becoming involved in deliberations on affairs of state and the promotion of Burgundian interests.

The standards for admission to and retention in the order were strictly observed. Proven military valor and honor were basic criteria for membership. Flight from the enemy (or even retreat in the face of greatly superior forces) and any violation of the code of military honor usually resulted in exclusion or expulsion. Chapters were supposed to be held every three years in late November on Saint Andrew's Day, when the record of each knight, including that of the duke himself, was subjected to close examination. When his turn came, each member would leave the hall while his conduct since the previous chapter was scrutinized and a decision taken whether to commend or to censure him. The records of these sessions show that among the causes for censure were overindulgence in female company, excessive addiction to pleasures of the table, haughty and overbearing behavior, and choleric displays. Undue attention to material benefits were frowned upon, and sloppiness of attire was not condoned. Exaggerated indulgence in practical jokes and coarse humor was also reprimanded. Penalties ranged from a dinner to be given by the culprit for the duke and his fellow knights to the supreme humiliation and disgrace of expulsion from the order. Expulsion could occur as a consequence of three kinds of lapses (1) heresy or doctrinal lapse—it was under this category that a cousin of Charles the Bold was excluded on charges of "sorcery and superstition" at the eleventh chapter held at Bruges in 1468; (2) treachery and felony, under which Philip of Crèvecoeur was expelled at the fourteenth chapter held at 's Hertogenbosch in 1481, for having sworn an oath of allegiance to the king of France; (3) flight or withdrawal in the face of the enemy on the battlefield— Louis of Chalon, prince of Orange, was refused admission at the first chapter at Lille in 1431 for having retreated before the French during a battle that year, even though he was held to be a courageous knight and had been admired for withdrawing his troops safely across the Rhône River in good order and with flags flying.

The investigation of the behavior of the sovereign of the order himself was conducted in the same manner as for the other knights, although it may be assumed that people exercised considerable care and discretion in the formulation of criticism. However, in 1468 and again in 1473, Charles the Bold was admonished on six counts and exhorted "not to plunge his people too quickly into war and to do so only after good and wise consultation; not to lose his temper; to moderate his language both toward his subjects and princes." It is recorded that Charles took this criticism in good part, but not that it had any practical effect.

The second article of the statutes stipulated that a knight of the Order of the Golden Fleece must give up membership in any other order, save in the case of emperors or kings, who could remain in an order of which they themselves were the sovereign. It was during the festivities for the creation of the order that Philip adopted his personal motto: *Aultre n'auray / Dame Isabeau tant que vivray* ("I shall have none other than Lady Isabel as long as I live"). Philip's personal conduct made a mockery of the statement, and some historians think that the last five words were a subsequent addition since only the first part was embroidered on the knights' mantles. According to this theory *aultre n'auray* referred solely to the second article of the statutes already mentioned.

The order's emblem was a gold chain wrought in the manner of the duke's device: a repeating design of intertwined steels (*fusils* or *briquets*) in the form of an ornate "B," for Burgundy, striking sparks from flints (*cailloux*), with a gold pendant in the form of a ram's fleece. This emblem, created by Philip personally, implied that opposition to Burgundy was an incendiary activity, as an accompanying phrase engraved on the collar made clear. *Ante ferit quam flamma micet, flamescit uterque* ("It strikes before the flame shines, and each bursts into flame"). The steel and flint in the collar also evoked the warlike ardor and valor which distinguished the knights. The collar had to be worn every day under penalty of having to pay for a mass as well as a fine. It could be dispensed with in battle but the fleece itself had to be displayed on the armor. This provision constituted an additional hazard for the knights who were thereby more easily identified by the enemy, from whom they could expect to receive special attention. The collar and the fleece remained the property of the order and reverted to it after death. It was not until the following century that it became permissible for the fleece simply to hang from a silk ribbon.

The last article of the statutes prescribed the number and the functions of the permanent officials. These were four in number. First was the chancellor, who had to be a high-ranking ecclesiastic of at least episcopal dignity. The treasurer was in charge of the relics, robes, documents, and armor, as well as the treasure of the order. The secretary, or recorder, kept two books in one of which were noted the qualities and praiseworthy achievements of the knights, while in the other were listed their errors and lapses together with any censures and penalties imposed. Finally, the king-of-arms, called "Golden Fleece," discharged procedural and diplomatic responsibilities.

After the year 1701 two Orders of the Golden Fleece came into being as a result of the struggle for the Spanish succession, one under the Austrian Habsburgs, and the other under the Spanish Bourbons. The present sovereign of the Austrian order is Archduke Otto of Habsburg. Its members forgather each year in Vienna for the statutory assembly, held on Saint Andrew's Day (November 30). The sovereignty of the Spanish order now resides in the person of the Infante Don Juan, count of Barcelona. In 1812, the duke of Wellington was admitted to the order by the Spanish branch as the first non-Catholic member. Since then the same branch has admitted other non-Catholic members, among them the emperor Hirohito and the duke of Windsor.

Until 1794, the treasure, the archives, and the armor of the order remained in Brussels, where the treasurer, chosen from the Belgian nobility, resided. In that year, the threat from the victorious French republican army prompted him to load all the property of the order on ninety carts which managed by a miracle to reach Vienna some three years later. The treasure and the rest of the material belonging to the order have remained there ever since and may today be admired in the treasure rooms of the palace.

CHAPTER VI

Tournaments and Banquets

Tournaments were originally associated with coronations and royal weddings. In the early Middle Ages they became primarily a testing ground for the strength and skill of the participants. The successful contender reaped the prize of individual fame and glory. In the course of the years, these knightly encounters acquired an increasingly decorative and artificial character. They became more elaborately staged and permeated with a romantic flavor, thus satisfying the thirst for erotic and dramatic expression for which the formal and traditional church plays were no substitute. In addition to the hostility of the church to tournaments, the nobility also incurred, but equally ignored, the condemnation of moralists and the derision of humanists such as Petrarch, who pointed out mockingly that none of the great figures of antiquity had engaged in jousting.

Knights wore the veil or some other article of apparel of the lady in whose name they entered the lists. Fanciful rules were devised which inflicted ludicrous penalties on those who were unhorsed, such as condemning a knight to wear a golden bracelet for a year or until he could find the fair holder of the key which would unlock it and set him free—on condition that he should place himself at her service.

These international knightly contests were made to order to serve the dukes' policy of organizing ostentatious and costly forms of entertainment.

In 1385, the double marriage took place at Cambrai of

John and Margaret, son and daughter of Philip the Bold, with Margaret of Bavaria and her brother William. This extraordinary event was celebrated in appropriate fashion in the presence of the young king of France, Charles VI, as well as the royal and ducal parents. After the wedding there was a banquet in the bishop's palace followed by jousting in the market place, in which the king himself and forty knights took part. One of these was declared the winner, and received as a prize a golden brooch set with precious stones "which Madame of Burgundy took from her bosom." The jousts lasted a whole week.

The Burgundian chroniclers loved to describe these dazzling encounters in great detail, as befitted their role of supporting everything which could enhance the fame of their master. By the late fourteenth century, these mock battles had become less dangerous to life and limb than formerly. Rules and regulations governing the weapons allowed, the armor to be worn, and the type and duration of the combat increased in clarity and number and were strictly enforced. The design of armor evolved continuously so as to afford better protection against the thrust of the lance and the blows of sword, mace, and battle-ax. For the greater part of the fifteenth century the leading center for the production of armor was Milan, until Maximilian I (who, through his marriage with Mary, daughter of Charles the Bold, had acquired the passion of the dukes for tournaments) drew off some of the best Milanese armorers and settled them in imperial cities like Nüremberg and Augsburg, where they founded a prosperous industry.

A tournament was announced sometimes as much as a year ahead of time in all countries where the institution of chivalry flourished, in the hope of attracting the widest and most skilled participation possible. All who declared their intention to take part were assured safe conduct.

The reinforcement of armor in the interest of personal safety gradually restricted the mobility of the contestant to the point where those taking part in a joust were turned into a kind of one-man horse-propelled tank, with a very narrow field of vision and only such personal mobility as was necessary to aim the lance at the opponent. By the middle of the fifteenth century, arms and armor for tournaments had become so specialized as to be markedly different from the equipment used for actual fighting.

A joust was a single combat on horseback fought with lances, usually with blunted tips, whereas a tourney, strictly speaking, was a group encounter between opposing sides, also on horseback but with the sword as the chief weapon. Originally jousts took the form of knights cantering ponderously at each other head on, thus frequently producing collisions with disastrous results. One of the most important innovations in the sport of jousting was the introduction of the "tilt" (derived from the French word *toile*, meaning "cloth") which hung from a taut rope strung down the length of the median axis of the list. It served the purpose of keeping the knights apart from each other and widening the angle of impact of the lance head on the armor. Subsequently, the tilt was made of wood to a height of some six feet. However, the practice of jousting without a tilt and with pointed lance heads (called *à outrance*) continued to be sanctioned for those who liked their sport tough, the chests of the horses then being protected with a heavy straw-filled mattress.

While the physical effects of being unhorsed were somewhat attenuated by the sand laid down on the ground of the lists, it is nonetheless astonishing that the contestants should usually have emerged unscathed from the impact of a fall in a suit of armor sometimes weighing as much as two hundred pounds. The horses, of course, did not always survive. In

1467, the Bastard of Burgundy jousted in England at a tournament organized by Edward IV. He had in his train twelve horses with trappings of gold and velvet cloth embroidered with the arms of Burgundy and the bar sinister "to show that he was a bastard," adds the chronicler rather superfluously, and hung with bells. He fought the queen's brother, Anthony Woodville, with both lance and sword. In a collision of the two horses in an open list, the Bastard's mount was killed, crashing to the ground on top of its rider. The contest was thereupon postponed until the next day. As the Bastard returned to his lodgings he said to the Burgundian chronicler who was covering the event for posterity: "Don't worry; today he fought an animal. Tomorrow he will be fighting a man."

Reflecting the trend toward the theatrical and away from the chivalrous tradition, tournaments tended increasingly to be supplemented by other attractions such as pageantry, sideshows, and banquets, held simultaneously. In 1428 the dukes of Burgundy and Brabant were matched against each other in Brussels ("in accordance with the advice of prudent counselors and heralds in order to avoid any accidents that might occur"), and on this occasion a number of masquerades were held in which ladies and gentlemen took part. Forty years later, on the occasion of the marriage of Charles the Bold and Margaret of York in Bruges, what was to be the last great festival of the Valois ducal court took place. It included both a banquet and the tournament. Thereafter, the duke involved himself too deeply in military enterprises to have time to organize festivities on a large scale.

Let us now take a look at a typical *pas d'armes*, or "passage of arms," as a tournament was called, which took place in the middle of the fifteenth century in the heart of the duchy of Burgundy. Such encounters, in the words of the Dutch historian Huizinga, were "based on a fictitious case of chivalrous adventure, connected with an artificial scene called by a romantic name." In this particular case the scene is laid in the year 1443, a few miles down the old road from Dijon to Nuits-Saint-Georges (now known as the Route des Grands Crus, because it passes through some of the greatest vineyards in the world), in the pleasant village of Marsannay-la-Côte, which today produces a well-known *vin rosé*. At the time of which we are writing, a tree grew there called "*l'arbre de Charlemagne*," perhaps because of its venerable age and great girth, which gave its name to a passage of arms minutely described by Olivier de la Marche. The date and place had long been proclaimed throughout the Burgundian territories and in other lands, all knights and squires qualified by birth to participate having been invited to do so. The challengers (those who had issued the challenge to all comers) were called *les tenans* (since they "held" the passage), while those who had accepted the challenge were called *les venans*, because they were "coming" to try to wrest control of the passage from the holders. The tournament thus represented an imaginary military encounter involving an attack against and a defense of a supposed position of strength.

It was organized by a Burgundian nobleman, Pierre de Bauffremont, lord of Charny, who had been captain general of the duchy, and who later married Marie, a bastard daughter of the duke. The preparations for the event lasted almost a year. Having selected twelve companions considered worthy of being invited to fight at his side, he issued a challenge to all comers. As a symbol of the challenge, each of the challengers wore on his left leg a silver knee plate, with a design of silver tears on a gilt ground for the knights and gilt tears on a silver ground for the squires. In spite of the unfavorable attitude of the church toward tournaments, the permanent planning headquarters of this particular enterprise was installed in the monastery of Saint Bénigne in nearby Dijon.

After many months, the time came for knights who had accepted the challenge to assemble at the appointed place in order that the details of the proceedings should be settled, in accordance with the number of knights and the kinds of combat selected. A low fence had been erected around the tree itself, and a tapestry with the coat of arms of the Charny family had been strung up against the trunk. Two shields, with the same heraldic motif of tears as on the knee plate worn by the challengers, but in the family colors, were fastened to the tapestry: the one to the right, with black tears strewn on a violet ground, stood for combat on foot, while the one to the left, with gold tears on a sable ground, signified mounted combat. Each visiting knight was invited to indicate which form of combat he preferred by touching one of the two shields with either his sword or his lance. Kings-of-arms and heralds of the lord of Charny stood guard by the tree and at a fountain in the vicinity, which the lord of Charny had rebuilt for the occasion in fine masonry. It was capped with a lofty platform on which stood statues of God, the Blessed Virgin, and Saint Anne. Against the sides of this platform were propped the thirteen escutcheons of the lord of Charny and his companions. A short way up the road toward Dijon a large crucifix of stone had been erected, before which was a kneeling statue of the lord of Charny wearing armor and helmet, and armed as for combat in the lists.

A little further along the same road, two lists had been built: one for combat on foot and another larger one for combat on horseback. Between them was a wooden structure from which one could watch what was going on in both lists. Down the center of the list for jousting was the tilt, and there were steps at either end to facilitate mounting and dismounting. On the side nearer to Dijon a large tent had been set up for the shelter and convenience of the challengers, while on the south side, toward Nuits-Saint-Georges, stood the lord of Charny's pavilion.

The foregoing suggests the labor and the expense of holding a *pas d'armes* in style. In addition to building the lists and the fountain and erecting the crucifix, housing had to be provided in the vicinity of Marsannay for the participants and their followers. Three nearby castles were made available for this purpose, furnished with all the staff, equipment, and provisions needed for their comfort, as well as food at all hours of the day. On this occasion, the lord of Charny kept open house for two full months to the admiration of the chronicler, who notes that he had never seen as much money spent over so long a period of time outside of a princely house.

When all the preliminaries had been completed, the duke of Burgundy, together with the duke of Savoy whom he had been entertaining, moved with their suites to Nuits-Saint-Georges some eight miles away, where they spent the night. The following morning, Thursday, July 11, 1443, the two dukes arrived at Marsannay-la-Côte at sunrise in order to be present at the first combat. There was great excitement because a Spanish knight, famed for his military prowess, named Pedro Vasco de Saavedra, had elected to touch both shields, thereby committing himself to fight both on foot and on horseback; and it had been decided that the lord of Charny himself would lead off on foot against him.

It is not difficult to visualize the scene that morning, aglow in the green setting of the vineyards and buzzing with the intense animation of last minute preparations in and around the lists. Marsannay lies on the western rim of the plain of the Saône, and it may be that the rays of the rising sun were burning off low-lying wreaths of mist, lighting up the bright colors of the trappings of the horses, tents, banners, and heralds' uniforms and striking sparks on the brilliantly polished armor. The air was loud with the voices and accents of many lands, the excited talk of the onlookers, the blare of trumpets, the clang of arms and armor, and the stamping and neighing of horses.

The two dukes entered the building from which they were to watch the action. The duke of Burgundy held a short white stick, to be thrown down by him into the list in order to separate the contestants and stop the combat when he felt that it had gone on long enough or if serious injury had been inflicted. About 8:00 A.M., the Spanish knight Saavedra entered the lists to present himself to the duke of Burgundy. He was dressed entirely in black and wore a short tunic and a small hat. Before him stood a member of the staff of the king-of-arms of the kingdom of Castille, who introduced him to the duke and asked him for permission to proceed, which being granted the Spaniard retired to his tent to arm himself. It was then the lord of Charny's turn to appear before the duke. The quantity and splendor of his equipment were in strong contrast to the soberness of that of his opponent. He was mounted on a horse decorated with his coat of arms, followed by six horses caparisoned with crimson satin and embellished with goldsmiths' work. His pages wore his colors, violet and sable, and he was preceded by his twelve companions, also on horseback, wearing the knee plate symbolizing the challenge on their left legs and sumptuously arrayed. In his right hand he held a small banner with religious scenes and he frequently made the sign of the cross. When he came before the duke of Burgundy, he dismounted and saluted him, addressing him in terms similar to those of his opponent.

Now came the choice of weapons under the supervision of

the marshal of Burgundy, who was ex officio in charge of the conditions under which the contests were to be fought. First, he asked the lord of Charny to produce the weapons to be used, for it was the custom that these should be furnished by the defending party. Two pairs of battle-axes and swords were thereupon handed to two kings-of-arms, who examined them minutely for length, weight, and condition in order to make sure that they were similar in all respects and that they conformed to the regulations governing the tournament— much as a referee nowadays examines the gloves in the ring before a fight. The Spaniard had the choice of weapons and picked the battle-ax. While these preliminaries were going on, kings-of-arms and heralds were clearing the lists of all those not personally authorized by the marshal of Burgundy or who had not themselves fought in a tournament. They also proclaimed that no one, whatever his or her station, should speak, cough, or make any sign whatsoever in favor, or to the advantage, of a contestant on pain of corporal punishment at the pleasure of the duke.

All this took up the best part of an hour and it was not until 9:00 A.M. that the two knights were ready for the fray. Only eight men in full armor remained within the lists, each one carrying a white stick but no sword. They were so placed as to be able to separate the contestants if necessary. The first to emerge was the Spaniard. He had removed the visor of his helmet, leaving his face uncovered, "and he stuck his head out of his helmet as though out of a window," noted the chronicler. When the lord of Charny entered the lists in his turn and saw that the Spaniard had removed his visor, he immediately raised his so that his face also was uncovered. Both of them made the sign of the cross before seizing their battle-axes. They then swung at each other and landed powerful blows up to the number prescribed by the regulations, at which point the duke threw down his white stick and the knights were separated by the men-at-arms. Thereupon they saluted the duke and offered to continue fighting at his pleasure, but he dismissed them. Neither one wished to leave the lists first, but it was decreed that since the lord of Charny was defending the passage, the Spanish knight should be the first to leave.

The two met again a couple of days later, this time on horseback with lances, and again honors were divided. They became fast friends as a result of their encounters, and Saavedra became a member of the duke's household with the very honorable rank of chamberlain. He won the confidence of the duke, for whom he later rendered important services both in the military and diplomatic fields.

The tournament lasted for six weeks, and the passage of the Tree of Charlemagne was successfully defended against numerous knights by the lord of Charny and his companions. When it was over, the two shields were taken down and hung in a side chapel of the church of Notre-Dame in Dijon.

In 1453, just ten years later, came the appalling news that Constantinople had fallen to the Turks. This caused general consternation in the West, although it could have come as no surprise to those who had been watching the growing Turkish infiltration of Thrace and the Balkans.

The duke formed a committee of three to consider the best means of stimulating and mobilizing the ardor, not only of Burgundian but of European knighthood, in support of a crusade. The highest officials of the Burgundian state, such as Chancellor Nicolas Rolin, First Chamberlain Anthony of Croy, and other dignitaries of the court worked closely with it. One of its members was the chronicler, Olivier de la Marche, who was to play a leading role in the ceremonies preceding the taking of the crusading oath by the duke and the nobility of Burgundy. It was decided to stage a spectacular series of tournaments and banquets, culminating in a feast to be held in the ducal palace at Lille. Their object was to have the greatest possible influence on the attitude of the lords and knights, and to win their support for the idea of a crusade.

According to an ancient custom, when noblemen wished to undertake a particularly hazardous or important action, they took their oath on a bird held to be noble by virtue of its nature and rarity, such as the peacock or the heron. For this occasion, the duke decided to take his oath on a live pheasant.

This choice, contrary to what is often assumed, was in no way a reflection of flippancy or levity on his part. Since classical times the pheasant was held to have spread into the Western world from the valley of the Phasis River (from which it derived its name) which flows into the eastern waters of the Black Sea just south of the Caucasus, in the ancient province of Colchis. It thus symbolized a link with the earlier "crusade" of Jason and the Argonauts which had inspired Philip the Good to found the Order of the Golden Fleece nearly a quarter of a century earlier. The duke attended the banquets and jousts in order to create the greatest possible excitement and sense of anticipation, and to emphasize the importance he attached to the whole enterprise.

The first of the series of feasts was a banquet also given at Lille by a nephew of Philip, Duke John of Cleves, on January 14, 1454. In the banqueting hall a prodigiously ornate set piece had been erected in the form of a ship under sail, in which stood a knight wearing the arms of Cleves. Before the ship was a silver swan with a golden collar to which was fixed a golden chain, as though it were towing the ship. On the stern was a miniature castle whose walls stood in the waters of a river on which a falcon floated. This display was an allusion to the origins of the family of Cleves: once upon a time, a swan had towed a ship containing a virtuous and valiant knight down the Rhine to the castle of Cleves. He had married the widowed princess of the region, and from this union the line of Cleves had since descended. The legend of the swan, which re-emerges in *Lohengrin*, was very popular in Flanders in the Middle Ages, when it was developed to the point of involving Julius Caesar's wife in a romantic affair.

During the banquet, a proclamation was issued to all princes, knights, and noblemen in the name of "the Knight of the Swan, servant of the ladies," informing them that he, the knight (Adolf, younger brother of the duke of Cleves), would be present in Lille on the day on which the duke of Burgundy was to hold his banquet, armed for the joust and prepared to take on all comers. He who was declared the winner by the lords and ladies present would be awarded the prize by the ladies: a golden swan on a golden chain from which hung a splendid ruby.

At the end of the banquet, the count of Étampes, cousin of Duke Philip, received the "crown of the Feast," signifying that it was his turn to host a banquet. It was held on February 5, and the duke was also present. It was now his turn to receive the "crown of the Feast," in the following manner. He was greeted by the Princess of Joy, "a very beautiful girl, young, aged twelve, dressed in a violet gown richly embroidered with gold, with Greek inscriptions on her flowing sleeves, and her head adorned with her beautiful blond hair" on which was a head-piece set with precious stones. She was mounted on a horse with blue silk trappings, led by three men on foot dressed in scarlet silk with small peaked green silk hats; and she sang a song composed for the occasion. Having reached the duke, she dismounted, climbed up a step onto the table, knelt down before him, kissed a crown of flowers which she had brought with her, and placed it on the duke's head, after which he raised her up and gave her a kiss before she took her leave.

On February 17, the day of the joust and the banquet given by Duke Philip, he and two of his sons, Count Charles of Charolais and the Bastard of Burgundy, flanked by a numerous and brilliant company, accompanied Adolf of Cleves, who was armed for the fray. The jewels which Philip wore on his hat were so many and so splendid that the chronicler's powers of description failed him and he admitted that the only words he could find were that they were fit for a powerful prince. Before this group went drums, heralds, and members of Adolf of Cleves's household, preceding a large swan with a golden collar in the form of a crown, from which hung a shield with the arms of the House of Cleves, as well as a golden chain whose other end was fastened to the knight's shield. The swan was flanked by two archers, who made motions as if to shoot at anyone coming too near the swan.

The trappings of Adolf of Cleves's horse were of white damask with golden fringes, as were those of his squire. He was flanked and followed by three young pages "dressed in the manner of angels," mounted on fine chargers caparisoned in white cloth. After them came a groom, dressed in white, on a small horse and leading a larger horse with white trappings on which the motto of Cleves was embroidered in large gold letters. The duke of Cleves brought up the rear in the company of John of Coimbra, grandson of King John I of Portugal, and a bevy of lords and knights all dressed in white and carrying lances.

The banquet took place at the end of the day, after the jousting was over. The huge window in the hall of the palace had been fitted with plain glass for the occasion. Three tables of different sizes had been provided for the principal guests, and there were five buffets for those who preferred to stand or whose rank did not entitle them to be seated. There was also a kind of grandstand for guests (some of whom had come from distant lands) to watch the proceedings but not to participate in the banquet itself. Many of those attending were in disguise.

The duke presided over the middle-sized table, and the count of Charolais over the largest one. The order of seating was somewhat strange. The duchess of Burgundy sat on the left of her husband and next to one of his illegitimate daughters. The wife of the Bastard of Burgundy also sat at the duke's table, while the Bastard himself graced the table of the count of Charolais with his presence. Nearby stood a high sideboard sparkling with gold and silver dishes and vases of crystal set with gold and precious stones. It was protected by a wooden barrier, being accessible only to those authorized to serve wine. On the walls hung a tapestry depicting the labors of Hercules, from whom the dukes of Burgundy claimed descent. The duke sat on a throne upholstered with cloth of gold shot with black thread, with a rich velvet border bearing his arms. Access to the hall was controlled by archers who guarded the five doors. Within, several knights and squires supervised the proceedings. In front of the head table was a pillar on which stood a statue of a nude woman with long hair reaching down her back and "wrapped in front in a cloth with Greek lettering in such a way as to conceal that which was appropriate." From the figure's right breast spouted a stream of hypocras (wine spiced with cinnamon, amber, almonds, and musk) while the banquet lasted. Near her, on a kind of raised stage was chained a live lion as the guardian and defender of the statue, and on a shield which rested against a nearby pillar was written in golden lettering,

"Don't touch my lady," perhaps an allegory of the lion of Flanders in the role of the protector of Constantinople.

A major attraction at banquets of this kind were the *entremets* (literally, "between courses," perhaps best rendered by the word "entertainments"). These fell roughly into two categories: (1) set pieces, with or without some form of activity connected with them, but remaining in one spot throughout the evening; (2) live acts, as in a music hall or circus, calculated to awe, amuse, and astound the audience. On this particular occasion, sixteen set pieces had been placed on the three tables: four on the duke's table, nine on that of the count of Charolais, and three on the small table. Before the ducal party entered the hall, persons whose rank or station justified it were admitted to gawk and gape at the fantastic creations which had been devised for the amusement of the duke and his guests.

Let us take a look, first of all, at what had been deemed worthy to grace the duke's table. There was a model of a church with glass windows, surmounted by a cross, solidly built and large enough to contain four singers and a bell which rang. Another "entertainment" consisted of the likeness of a small nude boy on a rock. From this figure there issued—as one writer delicately puts it—"a stream of rose water in the most natural manner in the world." Perhaps we may take this flight of the imagination to be the ancestor of the fountain of the *Manneken Pis* in Brussels. Then there was a galleon at anchor, laden with all kinds of merchandise with figures of sailors, some climbing up masts, others working in the rigging, and yet others carrying goods from place to place. Lost in admiration, the chronicler adds: "And it seems to me that in the largest galleon in the world there could not have been more activity, nor more varied kinds of rigging and sails than in this one." The fourth exhibit was a splendid fountain made of lead and glass, with small glass trees, leaves, and flowers of marvelous delicacy. And before it was a small meadow enclosed by rocks made of topaz and other exotic stones; and in its middle stood a statuette of Saint Andrew (the patron saint of Burgundy) holding his cross before him. From one of its arms spouted a stream of water a good foot high, which fell back into the meadow in such an ingenious way that no one could tell what then became of it; "however, it was nothing but pure spring water," comments a chronicler with a note of disappointment.

The second table boasted a pie large enough to accommodate within it twenty-eight musicians and their instruments; perhaps it lies at the origin of the old nursery rhyme:

> *Sing a song of sixpence, a pocket full of rye,*
> *Four and twenty blackbirds baked in a pie.*
> *When the pie was opened the birds began to sing.*
> *Was that not a dainty dish to set before a king?*

This was followed by a castle like that of Lusignan, the seat of the famous crusading family of the same name, said to be descended from the witch Mélusine, who was herself represented in the guise of a dragon—the form she took when professionally occupied—on the top of the highest tower. From two of the lesser towers of the castle, orange juice flowed down into the moat. Next to be seen was a windmill on a hill. To the top of the highest sail was fixed a pole on whose end sat a magpie at which people of all kinds were shooting with bows and crossbows, illustrating a proverb that it is a common (futile) occupation of men to shoot at magpies. Then there was a barrel in a vineyard, containing two kinds of wine, one good and the other bad. On it was the figure of a richly dressed man holding a sign on which was written, "Let him who wants to, take some." The fifth piece depicted a desert in which a tiger was fighting a dragon. Next came a savage riding a horse (others say a camel) which seemed to be in motion. Another proverb was illustrated in a piece representing a man beating a bush full of little birds. Nearby in an orchard enclosed by trellised roses sat a knight and a lady at table, eating the birds which the man was beating out of the bush; and the lady pointed with her finger to show that he was working in vain and wasting his time. We then see a madman riding a bear in a wild mountain landscape of different kinds of rocks covered with hailstones and icicles. The last entertainment on this table represented a lake, with towns and castles on its banks, on whose waters a well-equipped ship sailed in continuous motion.

The third and smallest table had three entertainments on it. The first was a tropical forest within which strange wild beasts moved and prowled as though alive. The second was a lion which moved about in a field; and there was a man before the lion, beating a dog, thus illustrating a Flemish proverb about how to master lions. The last piece showed a peddler walking through a village with a basket full of his wares.

Immense quantities of food were provided, each course consisting of forty-eight different dishes. Serving carts with the arms of Burgundy on blue and gold cloth, each one containing eighty-two pieces of meat, were lowered by pulleys from the ceiling.

When all the seats at the three tables had been filled, the bell in the church clanged loudly, whereupon three children concealed inside it sang a song, with a bass accompaniment. There followed a melody played on the bagpipes by a "shepherd" inside the pie on the second table. This was the curtain raiser for what can only be described as a program of vaudeville and circus acts, nine in all.

The first was a horse or a camel (both are recorded), which entered the banqueting hall backwards accompanied by sixteen horsemen. Two masked men were seated on it back to back sounding trumpets. After backing its way around the hall, it went out again. The organ within the church then played, and a very strange tune came from the pie, played on a German horn. Thereupon a wild boar, draped in green silk, charged into the hall with a monstrous figure on its back. The lower part of its body was that of an animal with hairy legs and the long talons of a gryphon; the upper part, in the likeness of a man, was clad in a green-and-white-striped tight-fitting jacket. He had a strange bearded face and carried in his hands two darts and a shield. On top of his head balanced a man in a crouching position, holding on to his shoulders. After this apparition had withdrawn, there was more singing in the church, accompanied by a flute and another instrument within the pie. Then, from behind a green silk curtain drawn across a stage at one end of the hall, four trumpets sounded a lively tucket. Suddenly the curtain was drawn, revealing the figure of Jason, the hero of the Golden Fleece, in full and shining armor, a sword at his side and a spear in his hand. From his neck hung a shield in the Spanish manner. Walking to and fro, he gazed about him uncertainly as though he were in unfamiliar territory. Rolling his eyes to heaven, he then knelt down and read a document which Medea had given him before he set out to conquer the Golden Fleece. On rising again to his feet, he was suddenly charged by huge and fierce bulls. Seizing his spear, he fought them, but they pressed hard against him in terrifying fashion, flames issuing from their nostrils and throats. Jason's spear thrusts and swordplay were much admired by the audience, we are told; but he seems to have made no headway until he suddenly bethought himself of a vial which Medea had given him, the contents of which were specifically designed to subjugate such bulls and to extinguish their fire. The treatment proved effective as prescribed, the bulls desisted, and the curtain was drawn back across the stage.

Again a musical interlude was heard from the organ of the church enlivened by a sweet-voiced trio's rendering of the song, "The Safeguard of My Life."

The next number introduced a wondrously large white stag with splendid golden antlers and a scarlet cloth on its back on which sat a boy of some twelve years of age, wearing a short crimson velvet robe, with a saucy black hat on his head, and handsomely shod. He grasped the antlers with both hands, and as he entered, he started singing a song called "Never Did I Ever See Anything Like It," while the stag provided a bass accompaniment on his own. We are told that this number found particular favor with the audience.

The church and the pie obliged once more with music ("the church and the pie always did something between two *entremets*," notes the chronicler).

It was now once again the turn of the stage with the four trumpets sounding and the curtain being drawn, revealing Jason walking around in full armor as before. He was suddenly set upon by a hideous dragon—and what a dragon! ". . . Its mouth and maw wide open, great red eyes and flaring nostrils, and so constructed that through its mouth and from most of its vents it ejected a stinking poison and amazing fire and smoke." The battle that ensued was so realistic that it seemed to the onlookers not to be acted but to be a bitter and deadly struggle. The odds seemed overwhelmingly against Jason until he suddenly recalled that Medea had thoughtfully given him a magic ring for just such an occasion. At the very sight of it the dragon gave up the fight, whereupon Jason cut off its head and pulled out its teeth, which he stored away in his game bag.

The next musical interlude by the church and the pie was interrupted by the sudden appearance of a burning dragon which flew almost the whole length of the hall and exited "so that no one knew what became of it." This feat was saluted by singing from the church and by the sound of viols from the pie, played by blind musicians.

Another aerial number followed: a heron taking to the air at one end of the hall was greeted by shouts from falconers, after which two falcons appeared, pounced on the heron, and brought it down to be offered to the duke.

After more music from the two usual sources, the trumpets heralded the reappearance of our absent-minded hero Jason, still in full armor, but this time plowing the land with a team of oxen. Turning them loose, he took the dragon's teeth from his game bag and sowed them in the earth he had plowed. As he did so, fully armed men sprang out of the ground and turned on each other so fiercely that blood flowed and they all killed each other in Jason's presence.

More organ music came from the church, but the pie ended the round one up, by offering the audience the sonic effects of a chase, "so that it seemed that little dogs were yelping and huntsmen shouting and horses sounding as though they were in a forest; and with this chase ended the *entremets* of the said pie."

We now come to the *pièce de résistance* of the program; first an act which Olivier de la Marche naturally takes a special delight in describing minutely. The other numbers, he writes, were but worldly, whereas this one seemed to him piteous and "the most special one of all, and so it was." A giant called Hans, whose name appears in accounts of several court festivities, entered the hall. He was said to be taller by a foot than any other man "without having recourse to any artifice." He was dressed in a long green silk robe with stripes, and he wore a turban after the fashion of the Moors of Granada. In his left hand he held a double-bladed ax, and with his right he led into the hall an elephant draped in silk. On its back was a castle in which stood a "lady" (Olivier de la Marche himself) impersonating the Holy Church, dressed like a nun in a robe of white satin under a black cloak and with a white kerchief on her head. As soon as she had entered the hall, she called on the giant to stop in order that she might address the noble company before her. The giant brought the elephant to a halt before the duke, whereupon the figure launched into a lengthy *complainte*, the gist of which was to implore the duke and his companions to come to the aid of the Holy Church, which was languishing and suffering in the hands of the infidels:

> *O thou, O thou, noble duke of Burgundy*
> *Son of the Church and brother to her sons,*
> *Hear me, and think upon my need.*
> *Let thy heart feel the shame and humiliation,*
> *The remorseful sorrows which I bear and feel.*
> *The Infidels, by hundreds and by thousands*
> *Are now triumphant in their curséd land,*
> *In which I once was honored....*

After this lamentation, a sizable number of armed men entered the hall, preceding the king-of-arms of the Order of the Golden Fleece, who carried a live pheasant wearing a golden collar richly adorned with pearls and precious stones. He was followed by two young ladies—one of them an illegitimate daughter of the duke—hand in hand with two

knights of the Golden Fleece. The duke, who, as the chronicler reminds us, had been briefed beforehand, looked at the
figure of the church with a compassionate expression, pulled
a document from his robe which stated that he vowed to come
to her aid, and handed it to Golden Fleece (as the king-of-
arms of the order was called). At this, the Holy Church gave
signs of great joy and thanked the duke, calling on those
present to follow his example. Thereupon the giant led the
elephant out of the hall again. The chronicler explains the
symbolism of the apparently incongruous presence of the
church within a castle on the back of such an exotic animal as
follows: The church had chosen to appear on an elephant as
a sign that she was having to face great and varied adversity in
remote lands. The castle stood for faith, while the giant with
the ax signified the church's fear of the arms of the Turks
who had expelled her and who were seeking to destroy her.

On that same evening and on the following day a great
number of oaths were taken by the noblemen present vowing
that they would participate in a crusade to free the Holy
Church from the infidel. However, many of the vows were
qualified and hedged about with saving clauses. That of our
friend the lord of Charny, who had held the passage of arms
of the Tree of Charlemagne, is a fair sample of the foregoing:
"I vow to the ladies and the pheasant, that if my very
revered and sovereign lord, my lord the duke, undertakes a
holy journey against the Infidels, I will serve him bodily and
materially, assuming that I shall not be ill or under genuine
medical care; in which case I shall send him eight or ten
gentlemen fully paid for one year."

After the tables had been cleared, and the company were
walking about, the chronicler writes that he felt as though it
had all been a dream. He then started thinking things over:

"The outrageous excesses and the expense of the banquets which had recently been held," with each one in competition with the others, "and in particular my Lord had put on such a show, spent so much money and invited so many people that I considered this to be an outrageous and unreasonable expenditure of funds, without sense except for the part having to do with the church and the vows following it; and even this noble undertaking seemed to me to have been launched too hastily." Chroniclers of this period being rarely given to experiencing twinges of social conscience, this passage is all the more remarkable. It suggests that Olivier de la Marche had been exposed to, or had overheard, criticism by others of the extravagance of this banquet and of its forerunners. Being largely responsible for that evening's proceedings, he would naturally be particularly sensitive to such criticism. He could also be expected to defend strongly that part of the program which involved the church, since this was his own personal contribution.

He goes on to describe a chance encounter with one of the duke's closest advisers, un-named but alleged to be quite well known to him, to whom La Marche unburdened himself of his personal misgivings. His friend undertook to explain and justify to him the reason for these festivities: they were the result of the firm decision and secret desire of the duke to carry out his intention, long held and set forth in the oath he had just taken, to serve Christendom and thwart her enemies. If it had not been for the insurrection in Ghent, he would already have put into effect the resolutions taken at the chapter of the Golden Fleece held at Mons a few years earlier. Thus he had long planned this series of events in order to encourage his subjects to come to the aid of the church in her distress. It is not—in the circumstances—uncharitable to speculate that the person quoted never existed, and that the chronicler ingeniously devised this means of disculpating himself on the record by laying the responsibility exclusively on the duke's shoulders.

The last formal event of the evening was a pseudoreligious torchlight parade with musicians playing drums, lutes, and harps followed by "God's Grace" in "a white satin dress very simply cut, in the style of a nun, over which she wore a long white damask cloak." She in turn was followed by twelve Virtues in "simple crimson satin dresses" with fancy hats, each one accompanied by a knight wearing a crimson tunic and a jacket of gray and black silk embroidered with a design of foliage and loaded down with jewels. God's Grace addressed the duke and told him that if he were to enroll the services of the Virtues in her train, he would certainly be victorious in his enterprise and would not only acquire a reputation in the whole world but also enter Paradise. Each of the Virtues then recited a verse in which she offered to serve the duke. When this rather pallid performance was over, all joined in dancing and feasting until nearly three o'clock in the morning.

Historians and critics in later times have tended to turn up their noses at what one of them calls "these barbarous manifestations of arrogant pomp . . . exhibitions of almost incredible bad taste." The trouble is that what may be bad taste and offensive to one period is not necessarily so to another. Entertainments of the kind described above might well appear "insipid and ugly" to some (though surely not to all) of us today, but they are a direct expression of the spirit of the period which produced them.

Critics frequently betray a feeling of frustration, even of irritation, at the contrast between the serene beauty of the paintings of the Flemish school under the Valois dukes and the extravagances of court entertainment. And yet the same artists worked at both, and there is no record of their sensibilities having been offended. The genius of the late Middle Ages, born of social and economic conditions which it is hard for us to imagine since they are beyond our range of experience, took forms responsive to the temper and the tastes of the times, achieving almost in the same breath both exquisite delicacy and beauty and what it may please us to dismiss as coarse and repulsive.

As for the reproach of extravagance, one minute's reflection on the way money is spent today on what generally passes as entertainment, with far less excuse, suggests that the court of Burgundy in the fifteenth century has nothing to fear in that respect from a comparison with the values of the affluent and permissive society of the twentieth century.

The Four Dukes

T HE four dukes pursued such a basically consistent policy that their images, historically speaking, have a certain uniformity which tends to overshadow their individual personalities. Whether we read about the activities of Philip the Bold or Philip the Good, of John the Fearless or Charles the Bold, we sense the same dominant urge and aim: the attainment of the goals of the House of Burgundy. Matrimony, wealth, the arts, political intrigue, and war when necessary were all harnessed to the chariot of the dynastic ambitions. If tactics and emphasis varied according to circumstances, the major theme remained the same. Thus their personal characteristics are, if not unimpressive, at least relatively unimportant in comparison with their ceaseless expenditure of energy in the service of their cause. "The whole history of the House of Burgundy," writes Huizinga, "is like an epic of overweening and heroic pride, which takes the form of bravura and ambition with Philip the Bold, of hatred and envy with John the Fearless, of lust of vengeance and fondness for display with Philip the Good, of foolhardy temerity and obstinacy with Charles the Bold."

That each of these four men possessed to an unusual degree both ambition and the means required to satisfy it is obvious. But is this all that is worth saying about them? Were they merely a monstrously developed expression of the meaner political and human characteristics of their age? Were they so obsessed with ambition and consumed by energy as to be entirely indifferent to people around them and devoid of any sense of social responsibility?

Their age was cruel. In war, towns and villages were burned down in revenge or as a warning, the population sent into the countryside to die of starvation or from the elements. Prisoners were often put to death. Innocent citizens were tortured and killed. A judicial duel to the death between two citizens of Valenciennes to decide a quarrel was publicized ahead of time like a sporting event and was attended by Philip the Good in person and by the nobility. It is described complacently in revolting detail by an eyewitness.

In Dijon, a popular institution called the *Mère-Folle* was permitted at certain times to turn the streets of the town into an uproar and to humiliate and persecute citizens considered guilty of unacceptable behavior. On one occasion, a wretched young woman who had married an old man in dubious circumstances was seized and beaten half to death in public, subjected to the most unspeakable humiliations, and finally burned naked at the stake after having been denied the last words of comfort from a priest.

What manner of men were these four princes? What do we know about them as human beings, apart from their role in events connected with their names and the flattery lavished on them by their hirelings? Incidentally, it is worth noting that many of the most detailed and matter-of-fact accounts of the cruelties and sufferings inflicted on individuals and groups in the course of events in which the dukes played a leading role were recorded by writers in the dukes' pay. One would have expected them to omit or at least to play down aspects of their masters' conduct which might be detrimental to their reputations and thus to their own interests, if recorded. The fact that they did not do so suggests that such conduct was then accepted as part of life.

We are fortunate in having contemporary likenesses of all four dukes. Philip the Bold is vividly represented in sculpture on the surviving west doorway of Champmol and in his funeral effigy, also at Dijon. There is also a portrait of him by an anonymous artist at Versailles as an older man. His features are heavy, with a massive jaw, but his eyes are keen. His sculptured representations give us no guide to his height. However, the kneeling effigy by Claus Sluter does not convey the impression of a tall man. The proportions of the head and arms in relation to the body suggest rather a stocky and powerful figure. The authoress Christine de Pisan, who had every reason to be complimentary about her patron, could not bring herself to flatter his appearance: "A man of dark complexion and ugly," she termed him. However, she praised his friendliness, his intellectual qualities, and his decisiveness. Froissart said that he paid great attention to important business and saw far into the future, a compliment the value of which is diminished by Froissart's practice of also applying it to others.

We know more about Philip the statesman, politician, and administrator than Philip the man. He was a diplomat rather than a soldier. While not an impressive military leader, he was, as were all his descendants, personally brave. He had won his surname as a boy on the battlefield of Poitiers by showing great courage in defending his father, and his role later in military expeditions sustained his reputation for valor. He delighted particularly in hunting and in sport generally, being especially fond of shooting with the crossbow. We have seen that like the other princes of the royal blood he favored the arts. His personal initiative in founding the charterhouse of Champmol was instrumental in establishing from the outset his dynasty's reputation of being enlightened as well as powerful. He was always keenly interested in crusading activities and was the prime mover in launching a crusade against the Turks which has been mentioned. His personal role in French political affairs has been generally condemned. He used and, in the judgment of most historians, abused his position in the last dozen years of his life as co-regent of France to promote his own political interests by raiding the royal treasury systematically and unscrupulously. Whatever his ethical shortcomings, he was a mighty builder who laid the foundations for the future strength of Burgundy and who won the admiration of his contemporaries for his political acumen and the brilliance of his achievements.

John the Fearless had much more to his character than merely "hatred and envy." His physical appearance is best conveyed to us by a portrait of him, now in Antwerp, which certainly suggests the presence of the vices attributed to him. The eyes, with a disquieting expression, squint downward along an interminable nose. The lips are pursed in a manner suggesting both harshness and obstinacy. The hands, with their long thin fingers, and thumbs turned back, are tense rather than at rest. History's harsh judgment of him is not unfounded; the assassination of his cousin Louis of Orléans, which he organized and cynically justified, began a sanguinary conflict of which he himself was ultimately a victim.

We know more about John the Fearless as a human being than we do about his father, whose policies he pursued unswervingly: the promotion of his personal and dynastic interests, the two being inseparable. Some seventy years after his death he is described as follows: "This duke John was very brave and stouthearted, and he was a shrewd man, filled with doubt and suspicion, who did not trust people. And for this reason he always carried a weapon under his robe and his sword was always girded on him, and he made himself feared and distrusted more than anyone." The list of his faults given by Richard Vaughan in his brilliant study of his rule is as impressive as the context in which they should be assessed is interesting, for although he was "violent, unscrupulous, brutal, and ambitious and hypocritical," we are also reminded that "in all this he was no different from the other rulers of the day." In fact, John was a deep and devious man whose complexity of character renders his human personality elusive.

His statesmanlike qualities sometimes form a contrast to his behavior. For example, he was approachable to others when he chose to be. He was not above showing respect for the opinions of officials around him, to whom he would occasionally defer. On the other hand, in spite of his scheming and deviousness, he has been described as totally lacking in prudence, as having been a "masterful opportunist who acted impulsively." This cunning, insidious man employed spies, had a passion for secrecy, conspiracies, and plots, used a bodyguard ("The Fearless" with a bodyguard!), and was apprehensive and nervous. These characteristics are a prefiguration of those of the "universal spider," Louis XI, half a century later. Fearful of his personal safety though he may have been, his surname was won by him on the field of battle; and his conduct as a young man both in the fighting and in the subsequent harrowing ordeals at the hand of the Turks following the catastrophe of Nicopolis show that he was possessed of exceptional physical courage and nervous stamina. How can we reconcile the characteristics of calculating shrewdness and devious scheming with imprudent and impulsive action? We simply have to accept the fact that these contradictions seem to have coexisted within him.

He proved himself to be a farsighted and sagacious administrator of his possessions, with a talent for imaginative and constructive reforms. He established special financial commissions and revised the fiscal system of Flanders. He re-organized his artillery, and revealed in general an ability in military affairs which may have owed something to the lessons so painfully learned in defeat at the hand of the Turks. According to Vaughan, "he became the only one of the four Valois dukes of Burgundy who really knew how to use an army," as he revealed in his campaigns and in a plan of battle which he issued. It is not surprising, however, that the good qualities he had could not outweigh the effects of the crime he had committed and his cynical behavior thereafter. The contrast between him and his father has been fully exploited by history, which has branded him a murderous tyrant, passing over in silence his achievements, thanks to which the interests of Burgundy prospered under him.

His reputation was naturally exploited by the "Armagnacs," as the partisans of the house of the murdered duke of Orléans were called. The text has come down to us of a letter addressed to him by the Devil himself, which was probably circulated by them as a form of political warfare. The fact that it was felt that such a document would benefit the Armagnac cause indicates how vulnerable was John's reputation. The letter contains the following picturesque passages: "Lucifer, emperor of the deep Acheron, king of hell, duke of Erebus and Chaos, prince of the Shadows, marquis of Barathrum and of Pluto, count of Gehenna, master, regent, guardian and governor of all the devils in hell and of those mortal men alive in the world who prefer to oppose the will and commandment of our adversary Jesus Christ, to our dearest and well-loved lieutenant and proctor-general in the West, John of Burgundy . . . .

"We pray and request, indeed we order and command, you to persevere, as you have begun, in obeying and carrying out the wishes of Satan. . . . Furthermore, we wish you to know that our court is completely void of devils in our service [because] they have all entered the hearts of your trusted people, accomplices and allies. . . . After you have carried out our orders in the area of your commission . . . we shall help you to cross the sea . . . and then we shall cause you to be crowned king of Turkey, emperor of Constantinople . . . , king of Jerusalem, Babylon, and Carthage and of several other kingdoms, both Christian and pagan. . . .

"In witness of this we have sealed these presents with our very horrible signet, present several troops of devils, in our most dismal consistory . . . in the year of our doleful reign six thousand, six hundred and six."

Contrary to what is often assumed, the arts continued to prosper under John the Fearless. He favored music at his court and pushed forward with the program of decoration in sculpture and painting at Champmol, Claus Sluter having died in 1406. Nor did he neglect the ducal library. Orders for illuminated manuscripts which his father had placed were completed, and the number of books was increased. He commissioned tapestries, among which was a set commemorating his victory over Liège when his personal courage had earned him his surname. He patronized writers (among them Christine de Pisan), as had his father. Like other princes of his time he liked to hunt, and he shared the prevalent extravagance of taste in the style and color of clothes. His private life was freer and more adventurous than that of his father. He was, it seems, "of a more amorous or wanton disposition," heralding the uninhibited licentiousness of his son.

The "Golden Age" of Burgundy is personified in Philip the Good. Under his rule of forty-seven years, his possessions enjoyed increasing prosperity, while the Burgundian state acquired and consolidated new territories.

His physical appearance is more familiar to us than that

of the other dukes. Several variants of a portrait of him by Rogier van der Weyden exist, the original of which is unfortunately lost. The most vivid impression of his personality is conveyed by the frontispiece miniature described in chapter IV. This is how he is described by his official historiographer, Chastellain: "In stature, he was a man of medium height; in weight in proportion to his height, with slight limbs, legs, and arms, though not to excess; he was particularly well favored in body, straight as a reed, with a powerful back . . . and well-set shoulders; his neck was in good proportion to his body. . . . [he was] thin of hand and neat of foot; bony rather than fleshy, with veins prominent and full of blood; his face was that of his male ancestors, of becoming length, dark of complexion . . . his nose was not aquiline but long; his forehead full and broad, not bald; his hair, between blond and black, was straight and flat; . . . he had thick and prominent eyebrows . . . his mouth was of normal size, his lips thick and high in color; his eyes were gray."

From his person radiated an aura of majesty: "No one other than an emperor or a king could aspire to such a manner as he . . . his mere appearance proclaimed him an emperor." He had the traditional courage of his breed; as a youth of nineteen he had wanted to fight at Agincourt, but his father had prevented him from doing so. He was proud and extremely sensitive. When he lost his temper, we are told, his eyebrows would protrude like horns, his features became convulsed, and he went blue in the face. Sometimes he would resort to violent action. On one occasion, after a quarrel with his son, he went off by himself on horseback into the forest near Brussels, lost his way, and spent the night in a humble wood-cutter's hut. Such fits of anger were fortunately rare, and he was easily pacified by a word of apology. Those who knew him best praised his moderation and temperance in his general comportment, in his clothes and at table, "where he ate slowly and cleanly." He had a horror of drunkenness. This show of propriety is in marked contrast to his private life. It was perhaps this outward pose of moderation and self-control which earned him his first popular surname of "*l'Asseuré*," or "the Self-Assured." Very soon after his death he was called "*le Bon*" in recognition of the improved conditions of life in the last thirty years of his role.

He was as pious as he was immoral, piety being one of the principal attributes of all true knights. He had masses said for the souls of any member of his household who died, however lowly his station. He was obsessed by the chivalrous ideal, outmoded though it was in his age. There is a touch of a late medieval Don Quixote in his general attitude toward life, in his insistence on personal exposure to danger, on loyalty, on truthfulness. The last particularly impressed his contemporaries: "Never, I believe," wrote Chastellain, "did a lie pass his lips, and his mouth was a seal and his words were as a document; [he was] true as fine gold and as whole as an egg." In other words, men thought they knew exactly where they stood with him, in contrast to what they had felt about his father.

He liked to mix with his people and to talk with them in their own houses. He had an instinctive sense of what others thought and felt. He took pleasure in grand entertainments and banquets. He was very fond of sports, particularly riding, fencing, jousting, and hunting. He also liked to read and to be read to, daily. His personal sobriety of dress was coupled with a passion for all that was most rare and precious, especially in precious stones, illuminated books, and tapestries. While he encouraged the art of music at his court, he does not seem himself to have been very musical. He does not appear to have been greatly interested in architecture.

His attitude toward responsibilities of state was somewhat aloof, for which he was reproached by his contemporaries. He considered himself to be above the task of counting his own gold and silver, and he despised financial and economic matters. He did not even care to know how much his fortune amounted to, and he disliked handling money. He had an unquestioning faith in the integrity of those around him.

Notwithstanding his occasional formidable outbursts of temper, his contemporaries stress the serenity of his temperament: "He bore with patience that which had to be," writes Chastellain, "and he was wont to shun melancholy and troublesome situations because he felt that they were harmful to man's existence and blinded reason." A whimsical side of his nature is revealed by what he did when his doctors advised him to shave his head following an illness. In order not to be the only one to go around bald, he decreed that all noblemen at court should have their heads shaved too, and more than five hundred noblemen followed his example "for love of the duke."

He disliked flattery and praise. He was not superstitious. Unlike his father, he had in him nothing of a calculating, shrewd politician. Historians differ in their assessment of his political role. Some deny him the qualities of statesmanship, greatness, and wisdom, seeing only laziness in his aloofness from affairs of state. The general verdict in his time, however, was that he was both a magnificent and a successful ruler, as the following well known passage from Chastellain shows: ". . . the distant parts of the world and the Sarrasin [Muslim] voices proclaimed him the Grand Duke of the West [literally, *du Ponant*, "of the setting sun"] because of the quantity of his lands, possessions, and domains all grouped together, which no other prince before him owned or subordinated to his authority, but only he . . . and because of several other peculiarities which raised him up and exalted him beyond the ordinary measure and condition of all other princes elsewhere."

His indolence of style did not mean that the interests of Burgundy were neglected. He was well served by an able corps of officials, above whom towers the figure of Nicolas Rolin of Autun, his chancellor for thirty-nine years. If one aspect of the art of ruling well is to know how to delegate wisely, then Philip the Good should be given credit for having entrusted the fortunes of Burgundy to his chancellor. The duke's intense sorrow when the news of his faithful servant's death was brought to him, when he himself was ill, is a moving tribute to the close personal ties which bound these two men, and reveals once again a deeply human and sensitive element in the duke's nature which helps to make him such an appealing figure.

A professor at a well-known English university is said to have opened a lecture on the last Valois duke with the remark: "Charles the Bold was a bloody fool," and this, in a nutshell, has been the verdict of history. However, even if Charles never realized that—in H. H. Munro's words—"the art of life is the avoidance of the unattainable," he cannot just be dismissed as a fool. Perhaps his English and Portuguese ancestry on his mother's side contributed to his moody and temperamental nature. His mother was the daughter of King John I of Portugal and great-granddaughter of Edward III of England. In a curious way, we seem to know more about his personality and less about him as a man than is the case with any of his forebears.

We know what he looked like from detailed contemporary descriptions and from a sensitive portrait of him, now in Berlin, variously attributed to Rogier van der Weyden or his school. He was of medium height (short by modern standards), of average weight, muscular, bowlegged from riding, with a stooped back and sloping shoulders. He walked with his head thrust forward and his eyes on the ground, which must have given him a wooden stride. He had thick, dark, curly hair, an olive complexion, a face more rounded than his father's, a straight thin nose, a strong chin, and a slightly prominent lower lip. The last has sometimes been considered to be the origin of this distinctive feature in the Habsburgs, but it seems unnecessary to look for this farther back than his son-in-law Maximilian, in whom it was well marked. His eyes are sometimes described as gray, sometimes as dark. To Chastellain, they seemed "gray, laughing, and angelically clear."

He was from his early youth headstrong and domineering. He loved sports and was a fierce competitor, renowned for his skill at archery and for his savage strength at the rough game of quarterstaffs. He shared the family fondness for hawking and hunting generally. Like most princes and noblemen of his age, one of his favorite entertainments was jousting. He was a reputed chess player—a new note at the Burgundian court, which may perhaps have been introduced by his mother's Portuguese entourage. In the years he spent in Zeeland and Holland (more or less exiled there by his father, with whom he did not get on well) he acquired a love of the sea and a romantic enjoyment of stormy weather. He was noted for his physical endurance: "I never heard him say that he was tired," writes Commynes, "nor saw him show fear."

In two respects, at least, he may have reacted consciously against his father's example: he was faithful to his wife (much to the astonishment and even concern of those around him), and he paid a great deal of personal attention to affairs of state and to financial matters in particular. His chastity may have also been induced by his reading of classical history, in which, notes the contemporary author Molinet, he had seen how "many powerful kingdoms collapse and stumble with their rulers in misery and ruin because of having too much indulged in the foolish delights of the female sex."

He showed much concern for the lot of the poor, to whom he was kind and generous as well as scrupulously fair in administering justice. The above qualities earned him the surname of *"le Travailleur"* or "the Industrious" during his lifetime, as well as *"le Hardi,"* like his great-grandfather. The surname of *"le Téméraire,"* or "the Bold" (perhaps better rendered by "the Rash," or "the Foolhardy") was only coined much later on and did not become generally applied to him until the early nineteenth century.

He seems to have been the most intellectually active of the four dukes. He was cultivated and eloquent. In fact he used to bore his courtiers with his orations. He knew English and liked to swear by Saint George when he considered it politic to do so. He also liked on occasion to impress his audience with the ardor of his feelings by using the phrase "we Portuguese." He prided himself on personal cleanliness and austerity, though he shared the traditional family passion for ornaments, costly jewels, and outlandish clothes. He was the most musically inclined of his line, composing, playing instruments, and spending much time listening to music. There is something ironic in the fact that although he liked to sing, he had a displeasing voice. He despised coarse entertainment. Although his very name is synonymous with military activity and is associated with cruel punitive expeditions against civilian urban populations, he was by nature chivalrous and did what he could to spare women and children in battle.

His greatest weakness was his pride, which prompted him to reject advice and to allow all opposition to exasperate him.

He was impulsive and aggressive by nature, and his violent temperament drove him sometimes to strike his soldiers and to speak so harshly to subordinates that, as has been noted, his fellow knights of the Golden Fleece felt constrained to bring this to his attention.

His contemporaries were quick to ascribe his thirst for glory to the tales he loved to read about the heroes of antiquity: "He yearned for great glory," writes Commynes, "which was what incited him to war more than anything else, and he would very much have liked to resemble those ancient princes about whom men have so much talked after their death."

He was religious, with a somber and fatalistic piety imbued with the spirit of the Old Testament. War and bloodshed were to him somehow inseparable from mankind's atonement to God for its sins, "for peace," in his own words, "is the gift of God, and he who owns land has war, and he who owns goods has lawsuits; thus it is for his own sins and for the sins of his subjects that there has to be war." Like his predecessors he was obsessed by the idea of a crusade against the infidel—what surer road could there be to immortal fame than the liberation of the Holy Places by a coalition of Christian forces under his personal leadership? But first he felt he had to settle accounts with his enemies nearer home and thus consolidate his domestic political base. This aim he was destined never to achieve. His first and foremost obstacle and enemy was the king of France. While there is room for a fairly wide range of opinions concerning the attitude of each of the first three dukes on Burgundian interests in relation to those of France, there is no doubt at all where Charles the Bold stood: he hated France and he hated Louis XI personally. A sense of humor is the last thing that comes to mind when we think of Charles, and the only known remark by him which contains even the hint of a smile concerns France; and it is characteristically icy, "as when the northern skies gleam in December." He loved France so well, he said, that he would wish her to be ruled by six kings instead of by one. He leaves us in no doubt about his goal: the creation of an independent kingdom of Burgundy, with its capital at Nancy, the capital of Lorraine, the elusive center of gravity of the Burgundian state, the bridge destined never to be built between its northern and southern territories, the very place where the dynasty of the Valois dukes of Burgundy was to be extinguished with his death.

Summary Chronology

(1363–1482)

1363 John II the Good, king of France, names his youngest son, Philip the Bold, duke of Burgundy.

1364 Death of John II the Good.

1369 Marriage of Philip the Bold with Margaret, daughter of Count Louis of Flanders.

1371 Birth in Dijon of the future duke John the Fearless.

1384 At the death of his father-in-law the count of Flanders, Philip the Bold inherits through his wife the counties of Flanders, Artois, Nevers, Rethel, and the Franche-Comté.

1384 The sculptor Claus Sluter is called to Dijon by Philip the Bold from Brussels in order to work on the decoration of the monastery of Champmol.

1386 Philip the Bold sets up at Lille a "Chambre du Conseil" the first organ of government for his northern possessions.

1390 Philip the Bold purchases the county of Charolais.

1396 Birth in Dijon of the future Philip the Good.

1396 Disastrous Franco-Burgundian crusade against the Turks (Nicopolis).

1404 Death of Philip the Bold, aged 63.

1407 Louis, duke of Orléans, is assassinated in Paris by hirelings of his cousin, John the Fearless.

1408 John the Fearless wins his surname after defeating the forces of Liège at Othée.

1415 King Henry V of England defeats the French at Agincourt.

163

1416 John the Fearless negotiates with Henry V.

1419 Assassination of John the Fearless at Montereau in the presence of the Dauphin, later King Charles VII of France.

1420 Alliance of Philip the Good with the English and the feeble-minded king of France, Charles VI, against the latter's son the Dauphin (Treaty of Troyes).

1421 Philip the Good purchases the county of Namur.

1422 Nicolas Rolin becomes chancellor of Burgundy.

1425 Jan van Eyck becomes a member of Philip the Good's household.

1426 Foundation of the University of Louvain by Duke John IV, of the Brabant branch of the House of Burgundy.

1430 Philip the Good (1) marries Isabel of Portugal, his third wife.
　　　　　　　　　　 (2) founds the Order of the Golden Fleece.
　　　　　　　　　　 (3) acquires the duchies of Brabant and Limburg.

1430 Joan of Arc is captured before Compiègne by Burgundian troops and is handed over to the English.

1431 Philip the Good acquires the duchy of Luxembourg.

1433 Birth in Dijon of the future duke Charles the Bold.

1433 Transfer to Philip the Good of the counties of Hainaut, Holland, and Zeeland.

1435 Peace treaty of Arras between Philip the Good and Charles VII. Under its terms Philip acquires the strategically important Somme towns, and the counties of Mâcon and Auxerre.

1453 Capture of Constantinople by the Turks.

1454 "Feast of the Pheasant" at Lille, at which Philip and his nobles take the crusading oath.

1454 Charles, count of Charolais, marries Isabel of Bourbon.

1455 David, a bastard son of Philip, becomes bishop of Utrecht.

1457   Birth in Brussels of Mary of Burgundy.

1461   Death of Charles VII. Philip the Good attends the coronation of Charles's successor, Louis XI.

1462   Death of Chancellor Nicolas Rolin.

1465   Death of Duchess Isabel of Bourbon.

1467   Death of Philip the Good.

1468   Treaty of Alliance between King Edward IV of England and Charles the Bold.

1468   Charles the Bold marries Margaret of York, Edward IV's sister.

1471   Louis XI declares war on Charles the Bold.

1471   Death of the dowager duchess Isabel of Portugal.

1473   Charles the Bold takes over the duchy of Guelders and the county of Zutphen.

1473   He meets the emperor Frederick III at Trier in the hope of obtaining from him a royal crown, but in vain.

1473   He creates central political and financial institutions for all his possessions (Ordonnances de Thionville).

1474   Charles the Bold visits Dijon and hints at an independent kingdom of Burgundy.

1474   Treaty of London between Edward IV and Charles the Bold, directed against Louis XI.

1474   Charles the Bold lays siege to Neuss on the Rhine.

1474   The duke of Lorraine and the Swiss Confederates declare war on Charles the Bold.

1475   Charles the Bold raises the siege of Neuss.

1475   Edward IV signs a separate peace treaty with Louis XI at Picquigny.

1476   Charles the Bold launches a campaign against the Swiss; is beaten at Grandson (March) and routed at Morat (June).

1476   He launches a new campaign (December) against the duke of Lorraine who had reoccupied his capital, Nancy.

1477   Charles the Bold is killed before Nancy (January 5).

1477   Louis XI occupies the duchy of Burgundy.
1477   Mary of Burgundy marries Maximilian, son of the emperor
       Frederick III.
1478   Birth in Bruges of Philip the Fair, father of the emperor
       Charles V.
1480   Birth in Brussels of Margaret of Austria.
1482   Mary of Burgundy dies from a fall from her horse.

Selected Bibliography

A. Contemporary Sources

For a survey of sources, see:

Vaughan, Richard. *The Valois Dukes of Burgundy: Sources of Information*, etc. Hull, University, 1965.
Three of the major French and Burgundian chroniclers of interest to us have been translated into English:

Commynes, Philippe de. *The Memoirs of Philip de Comines.* Ed. by A. R. Scoble. 2 vols. London, Henry G. Bohn, 1855–56.

———. *Mémoires.* Ed. by J. Calmette and G. Durville. 3 vols. Paris, 1924–25. Commynes was in the service of the dukes from 1464 to 1472, in which year he went over to Louis XI.

Froissart, Jean. *Chronicles*, etc. Tr. by Thomas Johnes. 2 vols. London, William Smith, 1848.

———. *Chroniques.* Ed. by J. M. B. C. Kervyn de Lettenhove. 25 vols. Brussels, 1867–77. His account ends with the year 1400 and thus covers all but four years of the lifetime of Philip the Bold.

Monstrelet, Enguerrand de. *Chronicle.* Tr. by Thomas Johnes. 2 vols. London, William Smith, 1840.

———. *Chronique.* Ed. by L. Douët d'Arcq. 6 vols. Paris, Soc. de l'hist. de France, 1857–62. His chronicle begins where Froissart left off and goes up to 1444.
The following are not available in English:

Chastellain, Georges. *Œuvres.* Ed. by J. M. B. C. Kervyn de Lettenhove. 8 vols. Brussels, Acad. roy. de Belgique, 1863–66. This account, which has unfortunately only partially survived, covers the years from 1420 to 1474.

Escouchy, Mathieu de. *Chronique*. Ed. by G. du Fresne de Beau-
court. 3 vols. Paris, Soc. de l'hist. de France, 1863–64.

Le Fèvre, Jean, lord of St. Rémy. *Chronique*. Ed. by F. Morand.
2 vols. Paris, Soc. de l'hist. de France, 1876, 1881. He was the
herald of the Order of the Golden Fleece, and he covers the
period between 1408 and 1436.

La Marche, Olivier de. *Mémoires*. Ed. by H. Beaune and J.
d'Arbaumont. 4 vols. Paris, Soc. de l'hist. de France, 1883–88.
His painstaking record of life at the ducal court deals with the
period between 1435 and 1488.

*For the personality, and the last two years of the life of Charles
the Bold:*

Molinet, Jean. *Chroniques*. Ed. by G. Doutrepont and O. Jodogne.
3 vols. Brussels, Coll. des anc. aut. belges, 1935–37.

B. Works of General Interest

Plancher, Urbain. *Histoire Générale et Particulière du Duché de
Bourgogne*. 4 vols. Dijon, 1739–81. The first major scholarly
history of Burgundy, based in part on contemporary documen-
tation and records.

Barante, A. J. P. Brugière de. *Histoire des Ducs de Bourgogne
de la Maison de Valois*. Ed. by L. P. Gachard. 2 vols. Brussels,
1838–40. Shortened edition by Y. Cazaux. Paris, R. Laffont (Le
Club Français du Livre), 1969. A highly readable narrative
account based on the chronicles, but historically unreliable.

Calmette, Jean. *The Golden Age of Burgundy*. New York, Mac-
millan, 1963 (translated from the French).

Courtépée, Claude, and Edme Béguillet. *Description Générale et
Particulière du Duché de Bourgogne*. First published in 7 vols.
between 1775 and 1785. A third edition, which is basically a
reprint of the 4 vol. 2nd edition of 1847–48, but with additional
material, including maps and an up-to-date bibliography, was
published by Editions F. E. R. N., 4 vols., Paris, 1967–68.

Drouot, Henri, and Jean Louis Antoine Calmette. *Histoire de
Bourgogne*. Paris, Boivin, 1928.

Kleinclausz, Arthur Jean. *Histoire de Bourgogne.* 2nd ed. Paris, Hachette, 1924.

Richard, Jean. *Histoire de Bourgogne.* Paris, Presses Universitaires de France, 1957.

C. Various Aspects of the Late Medieval Period, with Particular Emphasis on Burgundy

Cartellieri, Wilhelm Ernst Otto. *The Court of Burgundy.* New York, A. A. Knopf, 1929 (translated from the German).

Deuchler, Florens. *Die Burgunderbeute.* Bern, Stämpfli, 1963.

Doutrepont, Georges. *La Littérature francaise à la Cour des Ducs de Bourgogne.* Paris, Honoré Champion, 1909.

Huizinga, Jan. *The Waning of the Middle Ages.* London, Edward Arnold, 1927, and New York, Doubleday Anchor Books, 1954 (translated from the Dutch).

D. Northern Burgundian Territories and Zones of Influence

Frédéricq, Paul. *Essai sur le rôle politique et social des Ducs de Bourgogne dans les Pays-Bas.* Ghent, A. Hoste, 1875.

Kervyn de Lettenhove, J. M. B. C. *Histoire de Flandre.* 6 vols. (esp. vols. 4 and 5), Brussels, A. Vandale, 1847–50.

Pirenne, Henry. *Histoire de Belgique.* Vol. II., Brussels, Henri Lamertin, 1903.

E. Roles and Personalities of the Valois Dukes

Bartier, John. *Charles le Téméraire.* Brussels, C. Dessart, 1944.
———. *Charles le Téméraire.* Brussels, Arcade, 1970. (New edition, with numerous color plates.)

Bonenfant, Paul. *Philippe le Bon.* Brussels, Renaissance du Livre, 1955.

Hommel, Luc. *Marie de Bourgogne; ou le grand héritage.* 4th ed. Brussels, A. Goemaere, 1951.

Vaughan, Richard. *Philip the Bold.* London, Longman, 1962.
———. *John the Fearless.* London, Longman, 1966.

————. *Philip the Good*. London, Longman, 1970. These volumes, forming an invaluable history of Valois Burgundy, are particularly rich in bibliographies. The set is to be completed by a volume on *Charles the Bold*, to be published shortly.

INDEX

THE CENTERS OF CIVILIZATION SERIES, of which this volume is the twenty-ninth, is intended to include accounts of the great cities of the world during particular periods of their flowering, from ancient times to the present. The following list is complete as of the date of publication of this volume:

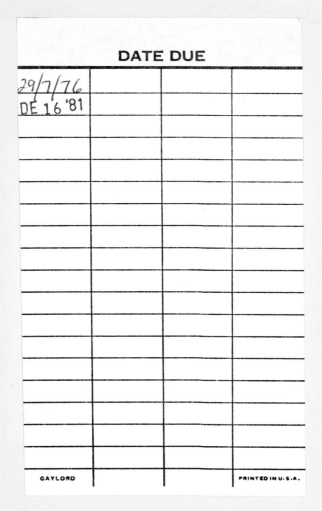

DATE DUE

29/7/76			
DE 16 '81			
GAYLORD			PRINTED IN U.S.A.